FIX-IT and FORGET-IT®

INSTANT POT COOKBOOK

100 Delicious Instant Pot Recipes!

HOPE COMERFORD

Photos by Bonnie Matthews

Good Books
New York, New York

Copyright © 2018 by Good Books, an imprint of Skyhorse Publishing, Inc.
Photos by Bonnie Matthews

Good Books books may be purchased in bulk at special discounts for sales promotion, corporate gifts, fund-raising, or educational purposes. Special editions can also be created to specifications. For details, contact the Special Sales Department, Good Books, 307 West 36th Street, 11th Floor, New York, NY 10018 or info@skyhorsepublishing.com.

Good Books is an imprint of Skyhorse Publishing, Inc.®, a Delaware corporation.

Visit our website at www.goodbooks.com.

10 9 8 7 6 5 4 3 2

Library of Congress Cataloging-in-Publication Data is available on file.

Cover design by Abigail Gehring

Print ISBN: 978-1-68099-431-5
Ebook ISBN: 978-1-68099-432-2

Printed in China

Table of Contents

Welcome to *Fix-It and Forget-It Instant Pot Cookbook* ❧ 1

What Is an Instant Pot? ❧ 1

Getting Started with Your Instant Pot ❧ 1

Instant Pot Tips and Tricks and Other Things You May Not Know ❧ 4

Breakfast & Breads ❧ 7

Appetizers & Snacks ❧ 31

Soups, Stews & Chilies ❧ 53

Main Dishes ❧ 95

Side Dishes & Vegetables ❧ 161

Desserts & Beverages ❧ 201

Metric Equivalent Measurements ❧ 220

Recipe and Ingredient Index ❧ 223

About the Author ❧ 228

Welcome to Fix-It and Forget-It Instant Pot Cookbook

Instant Pots have become a must-have for all households, and we knew you would want to see how Team Fix-It and Forget-It uses theirs. You'll find this cookbook to be full of easy recipes everyday home cooks can tackle with their Instant Pot. If you're new to Instant-Potting, just getting your feet wet, or are a total newbie, fear not! This cookbook has you covered! Even if you're a seasoned Instant-Potter, I'm sure you'll be thrilled to find some new recipes to add to your rotation of Instant Pot recipes.

Fix-It and Forget-It has always brought you recipes for your slow cooker you can make with confidence and ease. We are thrilled to be bringing you something new! We think you're going to love using your Instant Pot and can't wait for you to get started.

What Is an Instant Pot?

In short, an Instant Pot is a digital pressure cooker that also has multiple other functions. Not only can it be used as a pressure cooker, but depending on which model Instant Pot you have, you can set it to do things like sauté, cook rice, multigrains, porridge, soup/stew, beans/chili, porridge, meat, poultry, cake, eggs, yogurt, steam, slow cook, or even set it manually. Because the Instant Pot has so many functions, it takes away the need for multiple appliances on your counter and uses fewer pots and pans.

Getting Started with Your Instant Pot

Get to know your Instant Pot . . .

The very first thing most Instant Pot owners do is called the water test. It helps you get to know your Instant Pot a bit, familiarizes you with it, and might even take a bit of your apprehension away (because if you're anything like me, I was scared to death to use it!).

Step 1: Plug in your Instant Pot. This may seem obvious to some, but when we're nervous about using a new appliance, sometimes we forget things like this.

Step 2: Make sure the inner pot is inserted in the cooker. You should NEVER attempt to cook anything in your device without the inner pot, or you will ruin your Instant Pot. Food should never come into contact with the actual housing unit.

Step 3: The inner pot has lines for each cup (how convenient, right?!). Fill the inner pot with water until it reaches the 3-cup line.

Step 4: Check the sealing ring to be sure it's secure and in place. You should not be able to move it around. If it's not in place properly, you may experience issues with the pot letting out a lot of steam while cooking, or not coming to pressure.

Step 5: Seal the lid. There is an arrow on the lid between and "open" and "close." There is also an arrow on the top of the base of the Instant Pot between a picture of a locked lock and an unlocked lock. Line those arrows up, then turn the lid toward the picture of the lock (left). You will hear a noise that will indicate that the lid is locked. If you do not hear a noise, it's not locked. Try it again.

Step 6: ALWAYS check to see if the steam valve on top of the lid is turned to "sealing." If it's not on "sealing" and is on "venting," it will not be able to come to pressure.

Step 7: Press the "Steam" button and use the +/- arrow to set it to 2 minutes. Once it's at the desired time, you don't need to press anything else. In a few seconds, the Instant Pot will begin all on its own. For those of us with digital slow cookers, we have a tendency to look for the "start" button, but there isn't one on the Instant Pot.

Step 8: Now you wait for the "magic" to happen! The "cooking" will begin once the device comes to pressure. This can take anywhere from 5–30 minutes, in my experience. You will see the countdown begin from the time you set it to. After that, the Instant Pot will beep, which means your meal is done!

Step 9: Your Instant Pot will now automatically switch to "warm" and begin a count of how many minutes it's been on warm. The next part is where you either wait for the NPR, or natural pressure release (meaning the pressure releases all on its own), or you do what's called a QR, or quick release (meaning you manually release the pressure). Which method you choose depends on what you're cooking, but in this case, you can choose either since it's just water. For NPR, you will wait for the lever to move all the way back over to "venting" and watch the pinion (float valve) next to the lever. It will be flush with the lid when at full pressure and will drop when the pressure is done releasing. If you choose QR, be very careful not to have your hands over the vent as the steam is very hot and you can burn yourself.

The Three Most Important Buttons You Need to Know About . . .

You will find the majority of recipes will use the following three buttons:

Manual/Pressure Cook: Some older models tend to say "Manual" and the newer models seem to say "Pressure Cook." They mean the same thing. From here, you use the +/- button to change the cook time. After several seconds, the Instant Pot will begin its process. The exact name of this button will vary on your model of Instant Pot.

Sauté: Many recipes will have you sauté vegetables or brown meat before beginning the pressure cooking process. For this setting, you will not use the lid of the Instant Pot.

Keep Warm/Cancel: This may just be the most important button on the Instant Pot. When you forget to use the +/- buttons to change the time for a recipe, or you press a wrong button, you can hit "keep warm/cancel" and it will turn your Instant Pot off for you.

What Do All the Buttons Do . . .

With so many buttons, it's hard to remember what each one does or means. You can use this as a quick guide in a pinch.

Soup/Broth. This button cooks at high pressure for 30 minutes. It can be adjusted using the +/- buttons to cook more for 40 minutes, or less for 20 minutes.

Meat/Stew. This button cooks at high pressure for 35 minutes. It can be adjusted using the +/- buttons to cook more for 45 minutes, or less for 20 minutes.

Bean/Chili. This button cooks at high pressure for 30 minutes. It can be adjusted using the +/- buttons to cook more for 40 minutes, or less for 25 minutes.

Poultry. This button cooks at high pressure for 15 minutes. It can be adjusted using the +/- buttons to cook more for 30 minutes, or less for 5 minutes.

Rice. This button cooks at low pressure and is the only fully automatic program. It is for cooking white rice and will automatically adjust the cooking time depending on the amount of water and rice in the cooking pot.

Multigrain. This button cooks at high pressure for 40 minutes. It can be adjusted using the +/- buttons to cook more for 45 minutes of warm water soaking time and 60 minutes pressure cooking time, or less for 20 minutes.

Porridge. This button cooks at high pressure for 20 minutes. It can be adjusted using the +/- buttons to cook more for 30 minutes, or less for 15 minutes.

Steam. This button cooks at high pressure for 10 minutes. It can be adjusted using the +/- buttons to cook more for 15 minutes, or less for 3 minutes. Always use a rack or steamer basket with this function because it heats at full power continuously while it's coming to pressure—and you do not want food in direct contact with the bottom of the pressure cooking pot or it will burn. Once it reaches pressure, the steam button regulates pressure by cycling on and off, similar to the other pressure buttons.

Less | Normal | More. Adjust between the *Less | Normal | More* settings by pressing the same cooking function button repeatedly until you get to the desired setting. (Older versions use the *Adjust* button.)

+/- Buttons. Adjust the cook time up [+] or down [-]. (On newer models, you can also press and hold [-] or [+] for 3 seconds to turn sound OFF or ON.)

Cake. This button cooks at high pressure for 30 minutes. It can be adjusted using the +/- buttons to cook more for 40 minutes, or less for 25 minutes.

Egg. This button cooks at high pressure for 5 minutes. It can be adjusted using the +/- buttons to cook more for 6 minutes, or less for 4 minutes.

Instant Pot Tips and Tricks and Other Things You May Not Know

- Never attempt to cook directly in the Instant Pot without the inner pot!
- Once you set the time, you can walk away. It will show the time you set it to, then will change to the word "on" while the pressure builds. Once the Instant Pot has come to pressure, you will once again see the time you set it for. It will count down from there.
- Always make sure your sealing ring is securely in place. If it shows signs of wear or tear, it needs to be replaced.
- Have a sealing ring for savory recipes and a separate sealing ring for sweet recipes. Many people report their desserts tasting like a roast (or another savory food) if they try to use the same sealing ring for all recipes.
- The stainless steel rack (trivet) that your Instant Pot comes with can be used to keep food from being completely submerged in liquid, like baked potatoes or ground beef. It can also be used to set another pot on, for pot-in-pot cooking.
- If you use warm or hot liquid instead of cold liquid, you may need to adjust the cooking time, or your food may not come out done.
- Always double-check to see that the valve on the lid is set to "sealing" and not "venting" when you first lock the lid. This will save you from your Instant Pot not coming to pressure.

- Use natural pressure release for tougher cuts of meat, recipes with high starch (like rice or grains), and recipes with a high volume of liquid. This means you let the Instant Pot naturally release pressure. The little bobbin will fall once pressure is released completely.
- Use quick release for more delicate cuts of meat and vegetables—like seafood, chicken breasts, and steaming vegetables. This means you manually turn the vent (being careful not to put your hand over the vent!!!) to release the pressure. The little bobbin will fall once pressure is released completely.
- Make sure there is a clear pathway for the steam to release. The last thing you want is to ruin the bottom of your cupboards with all that steam.
- You MUST use liquid in your Instant Pot. The MINIMUM amount of liquid you should have in your inner pot is ½ cup; however, most recipes work best with at least 1 cup.
- Do NOT overfill your Instant Pot! It should only be ½ full for rice or beans (food that expands greatly when cooked) or ⅔ full for most everything else. Do not fill it to the max filled line.
- In this book, the cooking time DOES NOT take into account the amount of time it will take your Instant Pot to come to pressure, or the amount of time it will take the Instant Pot to release pressure. Be aware of this when choosing a recipe to make.
- If your Instant Pot is not coming to pressure, it's usually because the sealing ring is not on properly, or the vent is not set to "sealing."
- The more liquid, or the colder the ingredients, the longer it will take for the Instant Pot to come to pressure.
- Always make sure that the Instant Pot is dry before inserting the inner pot, and make sure the inner pot is dry before inserting it into the Instant Pot.
- Doubling a recipe does not change the cook time, but instead it will take longer to come up to pressure.
- You do not always need to double the liquid when doubling a recipe. Depending on what you're making, more liquid may make your food too watery. Use your best judgment.
- When using the slow cooker function, use the following chart:

Slow Cooker	Instant Pot
Warm	Less or Low
Low	Normal or Medium
High	More or High

Breakfast & Breads

Instant Pot Hard-Boiled Eggs

Makes 6–8 servings

Colleen Heatwole, Burton, MI

Prep. Time: 10 minutes   ❧   Cooking Time: 5 minutes   ❧   Setting: Manual
Pressure: High   ❧   Release: Manual

I cup water
6–8 eggs

1. Pour the water into the inner pot. Place the eggs in a steamer basket or rack that came with pot.

2. Close the lid and secure to the locking position. Be sure the vent is turned to sealing. Set for 5 minutes on manual at high pressure. (It takes about 5 minutes for pressure to build and then 5 minutes to cook.)

3. Let pressure naturally release for 5 minutes, then do quick pressure release.

4. Place hot eggs into cool water to halt cooking process. You can peel cooled eggs immediately or refrigerate unpeeled.

NOTE
from the cook
This is the easiest way to cook hard-boiled eggs for deviled eggs—which we prefer to call *angeled eggs.*

Instant Pot
TIP
Sauté cycle on my pot is very hot. Watch carefully or foods will scorch.

Poached Eggs

Makes 6–8 servings

Hope Comerford, Clinton Township, MI

Prep. Time: 5 minutes ⚶ *Cooking Time: 2–5 minutes* ⚶ *Setting: Steam*
Pressure: High ⚶ *Release: Manual*

I cup water

4 large eggs

1. Place the trivet in the bottom of the inner pot of the Instant Pot and pour in the water.

2. You will need small silicone egg poacher cups that will fit in your Instant Pot to hold the eggs. Spray each silicone cup with nonstick cooking spray.

3. Crack each egg and pour it into the prepared cup.

4. Very carefully place the silicone cups into the Inner Pot so they do not spill.

5. Secure the lid by locking it into place and turn the vent to the sealing position.

6. Push the Steam button and adjust the time—2 minutes for a very runny egg all the way to 5 minutes for a slightly runny egg.

7. When the timer beeps, release the pressure manually and remove the lid, being very careful not to let the condensation in the lid drip into your eggs.

8. Very carefully remove the silicone cups from the inner pot.

9. Carefully remove the poached eggs from each silicone cup and serve immediately.

Best Steel-Cut Oats

Makes 4 servings

Colleen Heatwole, Burton, MI

Prep. Time: 5 minutes   ♣   Cooking Time: 3 minutes   ♣   Setting: Manual
Pressure: High   ♣   Release: Natural

1 cup steel-cut oats
2 cups water
1 cup almond milk
pinch salt
½ tsp. vanilla extract
1 cinnamon stick
¼ cup raisins
¼ cup dried cherries
1 tsp. ground cinnamon
¼ cup toasted almonds
sweetener of choice, *optional*

1. Add all ingredients listed to the inner pot of the Instant Pot except the toasted almonds and sweetener.

2. Secure the lid and make sure the vent is turned to sealing. Cook 3 minutes on high, using manual function.

3. Let the pressure release naturally.

4. Remove cinnamon stick.

5. Add almonds, and sweetener if desired, and serve.

NOTE
from the cook

- Refrigerate leftovers in refrigerator.

- Nondairy milk is best because dairy milk can scorch. Additional milk can be added when eating if desired.

- This is supposed to serve 4 but rarely serves more than 2 at our house.

- We never add additional sweetener.

Fruit Breakfast Cobbler

Makes 4 servings

Hope Comerford, Clinton Township, MI

Prep. Time: 10 minutes ❧ *Cooking Time: 15–20 minutes* ❧ *Setting: Steam and Sauté* ❧ *Release: Manual*

2 pears, chopped

2 sweet apples, chopped

2 peaches, diced

2 Tbsp. maple syrup

3 Tbsp. coconut oil

1 tsp. ground cinnamon

½ cup unsweetened shredded coconut

½ cup pecans, diced

2 Tbsp. flaxseed

¼ cup oats

1. Place the pears, apples, and peaches in the inner pot of your Instant Pot, then top with the maple syrup, coconut oil, and cinnamon. Lock lid and set vent to sealing.

2. Press Steam and set to 8 minutes.

3. When cook time is up, do a quick release. When lid is able to be removed, remove the fruit with a slotted spoon and place in a bowl. You want to leave the juices in the inner pot.

4. Set the Instant Pot to Sauté and put in the shredded coconut, pecan pieces, flaxseed, and oats. Stir them constantly, until the shredded coconut is lightly toasted.

5. Spoon the shredded coconut/oat mixture over the steamed fruit and enjoy.

Serving suggestion:

This is very good with a little bit of whipped cream on top, or even as a dessert with some vanilla ice cream.

Cynthia's Yogurt

Makes 16 servings

Cynthia Hockman-Chupp, Canby, OR

Prep. Time: 10 minutes ⚜ Cooking Time: 8 hours+ ⚜ Setting: Yogurt

1 gallon 2% milk

¼ cup yogurt with active cultures

1. Pour milk into the inner pot of the Instant Pot.

2. Lock lid, move vent to sealing, and press the yogurt button. Press Adjust till it reads "boil."

3. When boil cycle is complete (about 1 hour), check the temperature. It should be at 185°F. If it's not, use the sauté function to warm to 185°F.

4. After it reaches 185°F, unplug Instant Pot, remove inner pot, and cool. You can place on cooling rack and let it slowly cool. If in a hurry, submerge the base of the pot in cool water. Cool milk to 110°F.

5. When mixture reaches 110°F, stir in the ¼ cup of yogurt. Lock the lid in place and move vent to sealing.

6. Press Yogurt. Use the Adjust button until the screen says 8:00. This will now incubate for 8 hours.

7. After 8 hours (when the cycle is finished), chill yogurt, or go immediately to straining in step 8.

8. After chilling, or following the 8 hours, strain the yogurt using a nut milk bag. This will give it the consistency of Greek yogurt.

NOTE

from the cook

Spoon yogurt into containers and refrigerate. I store it in quart jars.

Serving suggestion:

When serving, top with fruit, granola, or nuts. If you'd like, add a dash of vanilla extract, peanut butter, or other flavoring. We also use this yogurt in smoothies!

Carol's Yogurt

Carol Eveleth, Cheyenne, WY

Prep. Time: 10 minutes ❧ *Cooking Time: 15 minutes* ❧ *Setting: Keep Warm*

1 envelope unflavored gelatin
⅓ cup water
7½ cups 2% milk
3½ oz. vanilla yogurt
2 Tbsp. sugar

1. Soak unflavored gelatin with water.

2. Bring milk to boil in a medium sized nonstick pot on high heat (you can do this in the Instant Pot by using the Sauté function on high temperature).

3. Stir in the gelatin mixture.

4. Cool to near room temperature.

5. Add yogurt and sugar. Stir to mix. Divide the mixture into 4 pint jars. Cover with lids. (If you used the Instant Pot for these steps, clean it out, as it will be used in the following steps.)

6. In the inner pot, put all 4 pint jars in and cover with hot water. Close the lid and choose "Keep Warm" function for 15 minutes.

7. Let the pot stand for 10 hours closed.

8. Open the lid and take out yogurt. Cover with plastic wrap and chill a few hours before serving.

Instant Pot Applesauce

Makes 6 cups

Hope Comerford, Clinton Township, MI

Prep. Time: 10 minutes   ⚜   Cooking Time: 5 minutes   ⚜   Setting: Manual
Pressure: High   ⚜   Release: Natural

5 lbs. apples (whatever kind(s) you like), peeled, cored, and sliced

¼ cup water

2 tsp. vanilla extract

3–4 Tbsp. lemon juice

3 Tbsp. brown sugar

¼ cup or less of white sugar

¼ tsp. cinnamon

1. Place all of the ingredients into the inner pot of the Instant Pot and give a stir.

2. Secure the lid, making sure it locks and turn the vent to sealing.

3. Press the Manual button and set it for 5 minutes on high pressure.

4. When cooking time is up, let the pressure release naturally.

5. When pressure is done releasing, open lid, then use a potato smasher or immersion blender to make the applesauce as smooth or lumpy as you like.

NOTE
from the cook

You can leave the sugar out, or adjust the amount for your family's needs.

Apple Butter

Makes 6 cups

Hope Comerford, Clinton Township, MI

Prep. Time: 15 minutes ⚜ *Cooking Time: 60 minutes* ⚜ *Setting: Manual*
Pressure: High ⚜ *Release: Natural*

5 lbs. apples (about 15), peeled, cored, and sliced

½ cup brown sugar

¼ tsp. ground cloves

½ tsp. ground nutmeg

1 Tbsp. cinnamon

pinch salt

2 Tbsp. lemon juice

1 Tbsp. vanilla extract

¼ cup water

1. Combine all of the ingredients in the inner pot of the Instant Pot and mix well.

2. Lock the lid in place; turn the vent to sealing.

3. Press Manual and set to 60 minutes on high pressure.

4. When cooking time is over, let the steam release naturally.

5. Using an immersion blender, blend the apples until smooth.

NOTE
from the cook

This should keep in the refrigerator for up to 3 weeks in a tightly sealed container.

Cinnamon French Toast Casserole

Makes 8 servings

Hope Comerford, Clinton Township, MI

Prep. Time: 10 minutes ⚜ *Cooking Time: 20 minutes* ⚜ *Setting: Manual*
Pressure: High ⚜ *Release: Natural then Manual*

3 eggs

2 cups milk

¼ cup maple syrup

I tsp. vanilla extract

I tsp. cinnamon

pinch salt

16-oz. loaf cinnamon swirl bread, cubed and left out overnight to go stale

1½ cups water

1. In a medium sized bowl, whisk together the eggs, milk, maple syrup, vanilla, cinnamon, and salt. Stir in the cubes of cinnamon swirl bread.

2. You will need a 7-inch round pan for this. Spray the inside with nonstick spray, then pour the bread mixture into the pan.

3. Place the trivet in the bottom of the inner pot, then pour in the water.

4. Make foil sling and insert it onto the trivet. Carefully place the 7-inch pan on top of the foil sling/trivet.

5. Secure the lid to the locked position, then make sure the vent is turned to sealing.

6. Press the manual button and use the "+/-" button to set the Instant Pot for 20 minutes.

7. When cook time is up, let the Instant Pot release naturally for 5 minutes, then quick release the rest.

Serving Suggestion:

Serve with whipped cream and fresh fruit on top, with an extra sprinkle of cinnamon.

Quick and Easy Instant Pot Cinnamon Rolls

Makes 5 servings

Hope Comerford, Clinton Township, MI

Prep. Time: 5 minutes ⚜ Cooking Time: 13 minutes ⚜ Setting: Manual
Pressure: High ⚜ Release: Manual

2 cups water

17½-oz. can Pillsbury Grands! Original Cinnamon Rolls with Icing

1. Place the 2 cups water in the inner pot of the Instant Pot, then place the trivet inside.

2. Cover the trivet with aluminum foil so that it also kind of wraps up the sides.

3. Grease a 7-inch round pan and arrange the cinnamon rolls inside. Set the icing aside. Place this pan on top of the aluminum foil inside the inner pot.

4. Secure the lid and make sure vent is on sealing. Press Manual, high pressure for 13 minutes.

5. Release the pressure manually when cooking time is up.

6. Remove the lid carefully so that the moisture does not drip on the cinnamon rolls.

7. Drizzle the icing on top of the cinnamon rolls and serve.

Steamed Brown Bread

Makes about 10 servings

Carolyn Spohn, Shawnee, KS

Prep. Time: 25 minutes ⚬ *Cooking Time: 30 minutes* ⚬ *Setting: Steam*
Pressure: High ⚬ *Release: Manual*

I cup rye flour

I cup cornmeal

½ cup whole wheat flour

½ cup all-purpose flour

½ tsp. salt

2 tsp. baking soda

2 tsp. cream of tartar

½ cup molasses

2 cups sour milk (or buttermilk)

I cup raisins, *optional*

2 cups water

1. Prepare molds by generously greasing 4 pint-sized wide mouth canning jars (or 3 of the larger cans from canned fruit). You will need lids and rings for the jars.

2. Mix all dry ingredients thoroughly in a bowl.

3. Mix the molasses and sour milk in a separate, larger bowl.

4. Add dry ingredients to the liquid ingredients and beat well.

5. Place rack in bottom of Instant Pot inner pot and add the water.

6. Fill prepared jars about ⅔ full and cover tightly with greased foil. Place the inner pot on rack.

7. Secure the lid and make sure vent is set to sealing. Press the Steam function and set for 30 minutes.

8. Release pressure manually when cooking time is over, then carefully remove jars from cooker.

Serving suggestion:

Very good with Boston baked beans for an old-fashioned New England dinner.

NOTE
from the cook

1. For use later, cap with lids and rings. They will seal themselves.

2. Sealed jars will keep in refrigerator a week or more or can be frozen.

3. Cut bread by wrapping string around it and pulling up and across.

Appetizers & Snacks

Insta Popcorn

Makes 5–6 servings

Hope Comerford, Clinton Township, MI

Prep. Time: 1 minute ✣ *Cooking Time: about 5 minutes* ✣ *Setting: Sauté*

2 Tbsp. coconut oil
½ cup popcorn kernels
¼ cup butter
sea salt to taste

1. Set the Instant Pot to Sauté.

2. Melt the coconut oil in the inner pot, then add the popcorn kernels and stir.

3. Press Adjust to bring the temperature up to high.

4. When the corn starts popping, secure the lid on the Instant Pot.

5. When you no longer hear popping, turn off the Instant Pot, remove the lid, and pour the popcorn into a bowl.

6. Season the popcorn with sea salt to your liking.

Candied Pecans

Makes 10 servings

Hope Comerford, Clinton Township, MI

Prep. Time: 5 minutes ❧ *Cooking Time: 15 minutes* ❧ *Setting: Sauté and Mannual*
Pressure: High ❧ *Release: Manual*

4 cups raw pecans

⅔ cup maple syrup

½ cup plus 1 Tbsp. water, *divided*

1 tsp. vanilla extract

1 tsp. cinnamon

¼ tsp. nutmeg

⅛ tsp. ground ginger

⅛ tsp. sea salt

1. Place the raw pecans, maple syrup, 1 Tbsp. water, vanilla, cinnamon, nutmeg, ground ginger, and sea salt into the inner pot of the Instant Pot.

2. Press the Sauté button on the Instant Pot and sauté the pecans and other ingredients until the pecans are soft.

3. Pour in the ½ cup water and secure the lid to the locked position. Set the vent to sealing.

4. Press Manual and set the Instant Pot for 15 minutes.

5. Preheat the oven to 350°F.

6. When cooking time is up, turn off the Instant Pot, then do a quick release.

7. Spread the pecans onto a greased, lined baking sheet.

8. Bake the pecans for 5 minutes or less in the oven, checking on them frequently so they do not burn.

NOTE

from the cook

These can be kept at room temperature in a tightly sealed container (after completely cooled) for about a week. You could also store these in the refrigerator in a tightly sealed container for about 4 weeks.

Hummus

Makes 8 servings

Colleen Heatwole, Burton, MI

Prep. Time: 15 minutes ⚜ Cooking Time: 40 minutes ⚜ Setting: Manual or Bean
Pressure: High ⚜ Release: Natural

1 cup dry garbanzo beans (chickpeas)

4 cups water

2 Tbsp. fresh lemon juice

¼ cup chopped onion

3 cloves garlic, minced

½ cup tahini (sesame paste)

2 tsp. cumin

2 tsp. olive oil

pinch cayenne pepper

½ tsp. salt

1. Place garbanzo beans and 4 cups water into inner pot of Instant Pot. Secure lid and make sure vent is set to sealing.

2. Cook garbanzo beans and water for 40 minutes using the Manual high pressure setting.

3. When cooking time is up, let the pressure release naturally.

4. Test the garbanzos. If still firm, cook using slow-cooker function until they are soft.

5. Drain the garbanzo beans, but save ½ cup of the cooking liquid.

6. Combine the garbanzos, lemon juice, onion, garlic, tahini, cumin, oil, pepper, and salt in a blender or food processor.

7. Puree until smooth, adding chickpea liquid as needed to thin the purée. Taste and adjust seasonings accordingly.

Serving suggestion:

I serve with vegetable crudités, pita, or any crackers I have on hand.

NOTE

from the cook

This is one of my favorite recipes that I adapted for the Instant Pot. While I'm just using it to cook the beans it is still a great time saver. In this recipe, soft beans that would be considered overcooked in other applications are actually preferred.

Spinach and Artichoke Dip

Makes 10–12 servings

Michele Ruvola, Vestal, NY

Prep. Time: 5 minutes ☙ *Cooking Time: 4 minutes* ☙ *Setting: Manual*
Pressure: High ☙ *Release: Manual*

8 oz. cream cheese
10-oz. box frozen spinach
½ cup chicken broth
14-oz. can artichoke hearts, drained
½ cup sour cream
½ cup mayo
3 cloves of garlic, minced
1 tsp. onion powder
16 oz. shredded Parmesan cheese
8 oz. shredded mozzarella

1. Put all ingredients in the inner pot of the Instant Pot, except the Parmesan cheese and the mozzarella cheese.

2. Secure the lid and set vent to sealing. Place on Manual high pressure for 4 minutes.

3. Do a quick release of steam.

4. Immediately stir in the cheeses.

Serving suggestion:

Serve with vegetables, sliced bread, or chips.

NOTE
from the cook
Dip will thicken as it cools.

Creamy Spinach Dip

Makes 10–12 servings

Jessica Stoner, Arlington, OH

Prep. Time: 10–15 minutes & Cooking Time: 5 minutes & Setting: Bean/Chili
Pressure: High & Release: Manual

8 oz. cream cheese

I cup sour cream

10 oz. frozen spinach

½ cup finely chopped onion

½ cup vegetable broth

5 cloves garlic, minced

½ tsp. salt

¼ tsp. black pepper

12 oz. shredded Monterey Jack cheese

12 oz. shredded Parmesan cheese

1. Add cream cheese, sour cream, spinach, onion, vegetable broth, garlic, salt, and pepper to the inner pot of the Instant Pot.

2. Secure lid, make sure vent is set to sealing, and set to the Bean/Chili setting on high pressure for 5 minutes.

3. When done, do a manual release.

4. Add the cheeses and mix well until creamy and well combined.

Serving suggestion:

Serve with tortilla chips or bread.

Creamy Jalapeño Chicken Dip

Makes 10 servings

Hope Comerford, Clinton Township, MI

Prep. Time: 5 minutes ⚬ *Cooking Time: 12 minutes* ⚬ *Setting: Manual*
Pressure: High ⚬ *Release: Manual*

1 lb. boneless chicken breast

8 oz. cream cheese

3 jalapeños, seeded and sliced

½ cup water

8 oz. shredded cheddar cheese

¾ cup sour cream

1. Place the chicken, cream cheese, jalapeños, and water in the inner pot of the Instant Pot.

2. Secure the lid so it's locked and turn the vent to sealing.

3. Press Manual and set the Instant Pot for 12 minutes on high pressure.

4. When cooking time is up, turn off Instant Pot, do a quick release of the remaining pressure, then remove lid.

5. Shred the chicken between 2 forks, either in the pot or on a cutting board, then place back in the inner pot.

6. Stir in the shredded cheese and sour cream. Enjoy!

Blackberry Baked Brie

Makes 4–6 servings

Hope Comerford, Clinton Township, MI

Prep. Time: 5 minutes & Cooking Time: 15 minutes & Setting: Manual
Pressure: High & Release: Manual

8-oz. round Brie

1 cup water

¼ cup blackberry preserves

2 tsp. chopped fresh mint

1. Slice a grid pattern into the top of the rind of the Brie with a knife.

2. In a 7-inch round baking dish, place the Brie, then cover the baking dish securely with foil.

3. Insert the trivet into the inner pot of the Instant Pot; pour in the water.

4. Make a foil sling and arrange it on top of the trivet. Place the baking dish on top of the trivet and foil sling.

5. Secure the lid to the locked position and turn the vent to sealing.

6. Press Manual set the Instant Pot for 15 minutes on high pressure.

7. When cooking time is up, turn off the Instant Pot and do a quick release of the pressure.

8. When the valve has dropped, remove the lid, then remove the baking dish.

9. Remove the top rind of the Brie and top with the preserves. Sprinkle with the fresh mint.

NOTE

from the cook

I love to serve this at parties. It not only looks impressive, but it's so easy to throw together last minute.

Serving suggestion:

Serve with crostini, baguettes, or crackers. (Rice crackers are my favorite with this.)

Root Beer Chicken Wings

Makes 15–18 servings

Hope Comerford, Clinton Township, MI

Prep. Time: 2 minutes & Cooking Time: 18 minutes & Setting: Manual
Pressure: High & Release: Manual

5 lbs. chicken wings, tips removed and separated at joint

1 can (12 oz.) plus ¼ cup root beer, *divided*

¼ cup brown sugar

½ tsp. red pepper flakes

1. Place all the chicken wing pieces into the inner pot of the Instant Pot. Pour the can of root beer over the top.

2. Secure the lid and turn the vent to sealing.

3. Press Manual and set the Instant Pot to 18 minutes on high pressure.

4. Preheat the oven on broil.

5. When cooking time is up, turn off the Instant Pot and do a quick release of the pressure.

6. Remove the wings and spread them out on a baking sheet.

7. Mix together the ¼ cup root beer, brown sugar, and red pepper flakes. Brush this over the wings.

8. Place the wings under the broiler for 2 minutes.

Meatballs

Makes about 16 meatballs

Carol Eveleth, Cheyenne, WY

Prep. Time: 10 minutes ⚜ *Cooking Time: 20 minutes* ⚜ *Setting: Manual and Sauté*
Pressure: Low ⚜ *Release: Natural*

2 lbs. ground beef
1½ cups chopped onions
1½ cups bread crumbs
2 tsp. salt
½ tsp. black pepper
2½ Tbsp. Worcestershire sauce
3 eggs
8 oz. tomato sauce
1 cup water
3½ Tbsp. vinegar
3½ Tbsp. brown sugar
2½ Tbsp. mustard
1 Tbsp. liquid smoke
2 Tbsp. olive oil

1. Combine all ingredients, except the olive oil, in a medium bowl and mix thoroughly by hand.

2. Form into approximately 26 two-inch meatballs.

3. Coat the bottom of the Instant Pot inner pot with oil.

4. If you wish to brown the meatballs, turn on the Sauté function and brown on all sides, or brown in a separate nonstick pan first.

5. Layer the browned or raw meatballs in the inner pot, leaving ½ inch of space between them. Don't press down.

6. Secure the lid and make sure vent is set to sealing.

7. Set the Instant Pot to Manual and select low pressure.

8. Set the cook time to 10 minutes.

9. Once the timer goes off, manually release the pressure.

10. Remove the lid and serve the meatballs.

Serving suggestion:
Serve meatballs with barbecue sauce, if desired.

Porcupine Meatballs

Makes about 8 meatballs

Carolyn Spohn, Shawnee, KS

Prep. Time: 20 minutes & Cooking Time: 10 minutes & Setting: Meat
Pressure: High & Release: Natural

1 lb. ground beef or turkey

½ cup raw long-grain white rice

1 egg

¼ cup finely minced onion

1 or 2 cloves garlic, minced

¼ tsp. dried basil and/or oregano, *optional*

10¾-oz. can condensed tomato soup

½ soup can of water

1. Mix all ingredients, except tomato soup and water, in a bowl to combine well.

2. Form into balls about 1½ inches in diameter.

3. Mix tomato soup and water in the inner pot of the Instant Pot, then add the meatballs.

4. Secure the lid and make sure the vent is turned to sealing.

5. Press the Meat button and set for 10 minutes on high pressure.

6. Allow the pressure to release naturally after cook time is up.

Serving suggestion:

Very good on pasta or noodles with green salad and crusty bread.

Favorite memory of sharing this recipe:

My mom made these and they were a special treat.

Soups, Stews & Chilies

Chicken Cheddar Broccoli Soup

Makes 4–6 servings

Maria Shevlin, Sicklerville, NJ

Prep. Time: 15 minutes ⚜ *Cooking Time: 15 minutes* ⚜ *Setting: Manual and Sauté*
Pressure: High ⚜ *Release: Manual*

1 lb. raw chicken breast, thinly chopped/sliced

1 lb. fresh broccoli, chopped

½ cup onion, chopped

2 cloves garlic, minced

1 cup shredded carrots

½ cup finely chopped celery

¼ cup finely chopped red bell pepper

3 cups chicken bone broth

½ tsp. salt

¼ tsp. black pepper

½ tsp. garlic powder

1 tsp. parsley flakes

pinch red pepper flakes

2 cups heavy cream

8 oz. freshly shredded cheddar cheese

2 Tbsp. Frank's RedHot Original Cayenne Pepper Sauce

1. Place chicken, broccoli, chopped onion, garlic, carrots, celery, bell pepper, chicken broth, and seasonings in the pot and stir to mix.

2. Secure the lid and make sure vent is at sealing. Place on Manual at high pressure for 15 minutes.

3. Manually release the pressure when cook time us up, remove lid, and stir in heavy cream.

4. Place pot on sauté setting until it all comes to a low boil, approximately 5 minutes.

5. Stir in cheese and the hot sauce.

6. Turn off the pot as soon as you add the cheese and give it a stir.

7. Continue to stir til the cheese is melted.

Serving suggestion:

Serve it up with slice or two of keto garlic bread or bread of your choice.

Creamy Chicken Wild Rice Soup

Makes 4–6 servings

Vonnie Oyer, Hubbard, OR

Prep. Time: 15 minutes ☙ *Cooking Time: 15 minutes* ☙ *Setting: Sauté and Manual*
Pressure: High ☙ *Release: Manual*

2 Tbsp. butter

½ cup yellow onion, diced

¾ cup carrots, diced

¾ cup sliced mushrooms (about 3–4 mushrooms)

½ lb. chicken breast, diced into 1-inch cubes

6.2-oz. box Uncle Ben's Long Grain & Wild Rice Fast Cook

2 14-oz. cans chicken broth

1 cup milk

1 cup half-and-half

2 oz. cream cheese

2 Tbsp. cornstarch

1. Select the Sauté feature and add the butter, onion, carrots, and mushrooms to the inner pot. Sauté for about 5 minutes until onions are translucent and soft.

2. Add the cubed chicken and seasoning packet from the Uncle Ben's box and stir to combine.

3. Add the wild rice and chicken broth. Select Manual, high pressure, then lock the lid and make sure the vent is set to sealing. Set the time for 5 minutes.

4. After the cooking time ends, allow it to stay on keep warm for 5 minutes and then quick release the pressure.

5. Remove the lid; change the setting to the Sauté function again.

6. Add the milk, half-and-half, and cream cheese. Stir to melt.

7. In a small bowl mix the cornstarch with a little bit of water to dissolve, then add to the soup to thicken.

Chicken Vegetable Soup

Makes 6 servings

Maria Shevlin, Sicklerville, NJ

*Prep. Time: 12–25 minutes ⚜ Cooking Time: 4 minutes ⚜ Setting: Manual
Pressure: High ⚜ Release: Manual*

1–2 raw chicken breasts, cubed
½ medium onion, chopped
4 cloves garlic, minced
½ sweet potato, small cubes
1 large carrot, peeled and cubed
4 stalks celery, chopped, leaves included
½ cup frozen corn
¼ cup frozen peas
¼ cup frozen lima beans
1 cup frozen green beans (bite size)
¼–½ cup chopped savoy cabbage
14½-oz. can petite diced tomatoes
3 cups chicken bone broth
1 tsp. salt
½ tsp. black pepper
1 tsp. garlic powder
¼ cup chopped fresh parsley
¼–½ tsp. red pepper flakes

1. Add all of the ingredients, in the order listed, to the inner pot of the Instant Pot.

2. Lock the lid in place, set the vent to sealing, and press Manual, and cook at high pressure for 4 minutes.

3. Release the pressure manually as soon as cooking time is finished.

Chicken Noodle Soup

Makes 6–8 servings

Colleen Heatwole, Burton, MI

Prep. Time: 15 minutes ❧ Cooking Time: 4 minutes ❧ Setting: Sauté and Manual
Pressure: High ❧ Release: Manual

2 Tbsp. butter

1 Tbsp. oil

1 medium onion, diced

2 large carrots, diced

3 ribs celery, diced

3 cloves garlic, minced

1 tsp. thyme

1 tsp. oregano

1 tsp. basil

8 cups chicken broth

2 cups cubed cooked chicken

8 oz. medium egg noodles

1 cup frozen peas (thaw while preparing soup)

salt and pepper to taste

1. In the inner pot of the Instant Pot, melt the butter with oil on the Sauté function.

2. Add onion, carrots, and celery with large pinch of salt and continue cooking on sauté until soft, about 5 minutes, stirring frequently.

3. Add garlic, thyme, oregano, and basil and sauté an additional minute.

4. Add broth, cooked chicken, and noodles, stirring to combine all ingredients.

5. Put lid on the Instant Pot and set vent to sealing. Select Manual high pressure and add 4 minutes.

6. When time is up do a quick (manual) release of the pressure.

7. Add thawed peas, stir, adjust seasoning with salt and pepper, and serve.

Favorite memory of sharing this recipe:
   Chicken noodle soup is recipe I have served to my sisters.

NOTE
from the cook

Of course you can also prepare chicken for this recipe in the Instant Pot, but usually for this recipe, I use leftovers.

Asian Chicken Noodle Soup

Makes 4–6 servings

Carol Eveleth, Cheyenne, WY

Prep. Time: 15 minutes ❧ *Cooking Time: 10 minutes* ❧ *Setting: Manual*
Pressure: High ❧ *Release: Manual*

6 cups cooked chicken, cubed

1 medium onion, chopped

3 stalks celery, sliced

1 bay leaf

6 cups chicken broth

2 medium carrots, thinly sliced

1 medium red bell pepper, coarsely chopped

8 oz. rice noodles

4 cloves garlic, minced

2 Tbsp. reduced sodium soy sauce

2 Tbsp. finely chopped fresh ginger

½ tsp. sage

½ tsp. black pepper

3 cups shredded cabbage

3–4 Tbsp. rice vinegar

1. Put all ingredients into the inner pot of the Instant Pot.

2. Secure the lid on the pot. Close the pressure-release valve. Select Manual and cook at high pressure for 10 minutes.

3. When cooking is complete, use a quick release to depressurize. Press Cancel to turn the pot off.

Unstuffed Cabbage Soup

Makes 4–6 servings

Colleen Heatwole, Burton, MI

Prep. Time: 15 minutes   ⚜   Cooking Time: 10–20 minutes   ⚜   Setting: Sauté and Manual
Pressure: High   ⚜   Release: Natural then Manual

2 Tbsp. coconut oil

1 lb. ground beef, turkey, or venison

1 medium onion, diced

2 cloves garlic, minced

1 small head cabbage, chopped, cored, cut into roughly 2-inch pieces.

6-oz. can tomato paste

32-oz. can diced tomatoes, with liquid

2 cups beef broth

1½ cups water

¾ cup white or brown rice

1–2 tsp. salt

½ tsp. black pepper

1 tsp. oregano

1 tsp. parsley

1. Melt coconut oil in the inner pot of the Instant Pot using Sauté function. Add ground meat. Stir frequently until meat loses color, about 2 minutes.

2. Add onion and garlic and continue to sauté for 2 more minutes, stirring frequently.

3. Add chopped cabbage.

4. On top of cabbage layer tomato paste, tomatoes with liquid, beef broth, water, rice, and spices.

5. Secure the lid and set vent to sealing. Using Manual setting, select 10 minutes if using white rice, 20 minutes if using brown rice.

6. When time is up, let the pressure release naturally for 10 minutes, then do a quick release.

NOTE
from the cook

I use home-canned tomatoes in this recipe and break them up slightly in the pot. This is the equivalent of 2 15-oz. cans of store-bought diced tomatoes.

Favorite memory of sharing this recipe:

This is a recipe I have made fairly often, using moose, venison, or whatever ground beef our hunter son has given us. My husband likes any of these meats and much prefers this recipe to conventional stuffed cabbage.

Meatball and Pasta Soup

Makes 4–5 servings

Michele Ruvola, Vestal, NY

Prep. Time: 10 minutes ⚜ *Cooking Time: 9 minutes* ⚜ *Setting: Manual*
Pressure: High ⚜ *Release: Manual*

I cup diced carrots

½ cup diced celery

¾ cup diced onion

20–25 mini meatballs, frozen

1½ cups ditalini pasta

40 oz. beef broth

I tsp. salt

½ tsp. black pepper

2 Tbsp. diced parsley

2 Tbsp. diced green onions

1. Place all ingredients except parsley and green onions in the inner pot of the Instant Pot and stir.

2. Secure the lid, make sure vent is set to sealing, then put on Manual function, set to high pressure, for 9 minutes.

3. Use quick release to release pressure, then stir.

4. Top with parsley and green onions.

Split Pea Soup

Makes 3–4 servings

Judy Gascho, Woodburn, OR

Prep. Time: 20 minutes ♣ Cooking Time: 15 minutes ♣ Setting: Manual
Pressure: High ♣ Release: Manual

4 cups chicken broth

4 sprigs thyme

4 oz. ham, diced (about ⅓ cup)

2 Tbsp. butter

2 stalks celery

2 carrots

1 large leek

3 cloves garlic

1½ cups dried green split peas (about 12 ounces)

salt and pepper to taste

1. Pour the broth into the inner pot of the Instant Pot and set to Sauté. Add the thyme, ham, and butter.

2. While the broth heats, chop the celery and cut the carrots into ½-inch-thick rounds. Halve the leek lengthwise and thinly slice and chop the garlic. Add the vegetables to the pot as you cut them. Rinse the split peas in a colander, discarding any small stones, then add to the pot.

3. Secure the lid, making sure the steam valve is in the sealing position. Set the cooker to Manual at high pressure for 15 minutes. When the time is up, carefully turn the steam valve to the venting position to release the pressure manually.

4. Turn off the Instant Pot. Remove the lid and stir the soup; discard the thyme sprigs.

5. Thin the soup with up to one cup water if needed (the soup will continue to thicken as it cools). Season with salt and pepper.

Potato Bacon Soup

Makes 4–6 servings

Colleen Heatwole, Burton, MI

Prep. Time: 30 minutes ⚜ Cooking Time: 5 minutes ⚜ Setting: Manual
Pressure: High ⚜ Release: Manual

5 lbs. potatoes, peeled and cubed

3 stalks of celery, diced into roughly ¼- to ½-inch pieces

1 large onion, chopped

1 clove garlic, minced

1 Tbsp. seasoning salt

½ tsp. black pepper

4 cups chicken broth

1 lb. bacon, fried crisp and rough chopped

1 cup half-and-half

1 cup milk, 2% or whole

sour cream, shredded cheddar cheese, and diced green onion to garnish, *optional*

1. Place potatoes in bottom of the Instant Pot inner pot.

2. Add celery, onion, garlic, seasoning salt, and pepper, then stir to combine.

3. Add chicken broth and bacon to pot and stir to combine.

4. Secure the lid and make sure vent is in the sealing position. Using Manual mode select 5 minutes, high pressure.

5. Manually release the pressure when cooking time is up. Open pot and roughly mash potatoes, leaving some large chunks if desired.

6. Add half-and-half and milk.

7. Serve while still hot with desired assortment of garnishes.

NOTE
from the cook

• I like this recipe because it requires no sautéing of onion, garlic, or celery but still tastes good.

• I have used a variety of potatoes for this recipe. We raise mostly Kennebec but also red potatoes. My spouse likes this recipe with either.

Split Pea Soup with Chicken Sausage

Makes 4–6 servings

Colleen Heatwole, Burton, MI

Prep. Time: 15 minutes & Cooking Time: 10 minutes & Setting: Sauté and Manual
Pressure: High & Release: Natural then Manual

1 lb. ground chicken sausage
2 Tbsp. oil
1 medium onion, finely chopped
1 medium carrot, peeled and diced
1 stalk celery, diced
2 cloves garlic, minced
32 oz. chicken stock
2 cups water
16-oz. package split peas, sorted and rinsed
¼ tsp. dry red pepper flakes
½ cup half-and-half or whole milk
salt and fresh ground pepper to taste

1. Using Sauté function brown sausage in the inner pot of the Instant Pot. Remove to platter or bowl.

2. Heat the oil in the inner pot of the Instant Pot using Sauté function.

3. Sauté onion, celery, and carrot until tender, about 5 minutes.

4. Add garlic and sauté additional minute.

5. Add chicken stock, water, split peas, and red pepper flakes.

6. Secure lid and make sure vent is pointing to sealing. Using Manual mode, select 10 minutes cook time, high pressure.

7. When cook time is up, let the pressure release naturally for 10 minutes, then release the rest of the pressure manually.

8. Using immersion blender or food processor, puree the contents of the inner pot until mixture is very smooth.

9. Select Sauté and add sausage and half-and-half; heat until sausage is heated through.

10. Add salt and pepper to taste.

Potato Soup

Makes 4 servings

Michele Ruvola, Vestal, NY

Prep. Time: 20 minutes ⚭ *Cooking Time: 5 minutes* ⚭ *Setting: Manual*
Pressure: High ⚭ *Release: Manual*

5 lbs. russet potatoes, peeled and cubed

3 stalks celery, sliced thin

1 large onion, diced

1 clove garlic, minced

1 Tbsp. seasoning salt

1 tsp. ground black pepper

¼ cup butter

1 lb. bacon, fried crisp, rough chopped

4 cups chicken stock

1 cup heavy cream

½ cup whole milk

Sour cream, shredded cheddar cheese, sliced green onions for garnish, *optional*

1. Put potatoes, celery, onion, garlic, seasoning salt, pepper and butter in the inner pot of the Instant Pot. Stir to combine.

2. Add bacon and chicken stock, then stir to combine.

3. Secure the lid and make sure the vent is on sealing. Push the Manual mode button, then set timer for 5 minutes on high pressure.

4. Quick release the steam when cook time is up.

5. Remove lid; mash potatoes to make a semi-smooth soup.

6. Add cream and milk; stir to combine.

7. Serve with garnishes if desired.

Serving Suggestion:

Perfect on a cold night with slices of bread on the side or a salad.

Brown Lentil Soup

Makes 3–5 servings

Colleen Heatwole, Burton, MI

Prep. Time: 15 minutes ⚘ *Cooking Time: 20 minutes* ⚘ *Setting: Sauté and Manual*
Pressure: High ⚘ *Release: Manual*

1 medium onion, chopped

1 Tbsp. olive oil

1 medium carrot, diced

2 cloves garlic, minced

1 small bay leaf

1 pound brown lentils

5 cups chicken broth

1 tsp. salt

¼ tsp. ground black pepper

½ tsp. lemon juice

1. Using the Sauté function, sauté the chopped onion in oil in the inner pot of the Instant Pot about 2 minutes, or until it starts to soften.

2. Add diced carrot and sauté 3 minutes more until it begins to soften. Stir frequently or it will stick.

3. Add garlic and sauté 1 more minute.

4. Add bay leaf, lentils, and broth to pot.

5. Secure the lid and make sure vent is at sealing. Using Manual setting, select 14 minutes and cook on high pressure.

6. When cooking time is up, do a quick release of the pressure.

7. Discard bay leaf.

8. Stir in salt, pepper, and lemon juice, then adjust seasonings to taste.

Instant Pot TIPS

When I'm using quick release, I often carry my pot to the garage just a few steps away, and cover the vent with a towel while I switch from sealing to venting.

Butternut Squash Soup

Makes 4 servings

Colleen Heatwole, Burton, MI

Prep. Time: 30 minutes ❧ Cooking Time: 15 minutes ❧ Setting: Sauté and Manual
Pressure: High ❧ Release: Manual

2 Tbsp. butter

1 large onion, chopped

2 cloves garlic, minced

1 tsp. thyme

½ tsp. sage

salt and pepper to taste

2 large butternut squash, peeled, seeded, and cubed (about 4 pounds)

4 cups chicken stock

1. In the inner pot of the Instant Pot, melt the butter using sauté function.

2. Add onion and garlic and cook until soft, 3 to 5 minutes.

3. Add thyme and sage and cook another minute. Season with salt and pepper.

4. Stir in butternut squash and add chicken stock.

5. Secure the lid and make sure vent is at sealing. Using Manual setting, cook squash and seasonings 10 minutes, using high pressure.

6. When time is up, do a quick release of the pressure.

7. Puree the soup in a food processor or use immersion blender right in the inner pot. If soup is too thick, add more stock. Adjust salt and pepper as needed.

Favorite memory of sharing this recipe:

I served my sisters this dish for the evening meal prior to a Thanksgiving feast the next day. It was well received.

NOTE
from the cook

• Amount of salt needed or used in cooking is definitely a matter of taste and preference. I prefer and use much less salt and pepper than does my husband, so the final seasoning adjustment is always at the table where he adds more and I add none.

• The most time-consuming part of this recipe is cutting up the squash. My husband usually does that for me.

Black Bean Soup

Makes 4–6 servings

Colleen Heatwole, Burton, MI

Prep. Time: 20 minutes ⚜ *Cooking Time: 25 minutes (unless beans have been soaked)*
Setting: Sauté and Bean/Chili ⚜ *Pressure: High* ⚜ *Release: Natural*

2 Tbsp. coconut oil

I cup coarsely chopped onion

2 cups dry black beans, cleaned of debris and rinsed

6 cups vegetable or chicken broth

3 cloves garlic, minced

½ tsp. paprika

⅛ tsp. red pepper flakes

2 large bay leaves

I tsp. cumin

2 tsp. oregano

½ tsp. salt (more if desired)

yogurt, sour cream for garnish, *optional*

1. Heat the oil in the inner pot of the Instant Pot with the sauté function. Add onion and sauté 2 minutes.

2. Add remaining ingredients except garnishes, and stir well.

3. Secure lid and make sure vent is at sealing, then set to Bean/Chili for 25 minutes.

4. After time is up let pressure release naturally.

5. Remove bay leaves and serve with desired garnishes.

> Instant Pot
> ## TIPS
> I rarely presoak beans, but cooking time can be decreased if you remember to do so.

Ground Turkey Stew

Makes 4–6 servings

Carol Eveleth, Cheyenne, WY

Prep. Time: 5 minutes ♣ *Cooking Time: 25 minutes* ♣ *Setting: Manual*
Pressure: High ♣ *Release: Manual*

1 Tbsp. oil

1 onion, chopped

1 lb. ground turkey

½ tsp. garlic powder

1 tsp. chili powder

¾ tsp. cumin

2 tsp. coriander

1 tsp. dried oregano

½ tsp. salt

1 green pepper, chopped

1 red pepper, chopped

1 tomato, chopped

1½ cups tomato sauce

1 Tbsp. soy sauce

1 cup water

2 handfuls cilantro, chopped

15-oz. can black beans

1. Press the Sauté function on the control panel of the Instant Pot.

2. Add the oil to the inner pot and let it get hot. Add onion, season with salt, and sauté for a few minutes, or until light golden.

3. Add ground turkey. Break the ground meat using a wooden spoon to avoid formation of lumps. Sauté for a few minutes, until the pink color has faded.

4. Add garlic powder, chili powder, cumin, coriander, dried oregano, and salt. Combine well. Add green pepper, red pepper, and chopped tomato. Combine well.

5. Add tomato sauce, soy sauce, and water; combine well.

6. Close and secure the lid. Click on the Cancel key to cancel the Sauté mode. Make sure the pressure release valve on the lid is in the sealing position.

7. Click on Manual function first and then select high pressure. Click the + button and set the time to 15 minutes.

8. You can either have the steam release naturally (it will take around 20 minutes) or, after 10 minutes, turn the pressure release valve on the lid to venting and release steam. Be careful as the steam is very hot. After the pressure has released completely, open the lid.

9. If the stew is watery, turn on the Sauté function and let it cook for a few more minutes with the lid off.

10. Add cilantro and can of black beans, combine well, and let cook for a few minutes.

Serving suggestion:

You can serve this with pasta—add pasta into a bowl and add cheddar cheese on top.

NOTE

from the cook

This also works well with ground beef.

Beef Stew

Makes 6 servings

Carol Eveleth, Cheyenne, WY

Prep. Time: 10 minutes & Cooking Time: 65 minutes & Setting: Sauté and Manual
Pressure: High & Release: Manual

2 lbs. chuck steak, 1½-inch thickness

2 tsp. salt or to taste

½ tsp. black pepper

1 Tbsp. Worcestershire sauce

1 Tbsp. light soy sauce

3 Tbsp. tomato paste

1½ cups low-sodium chicken stock

12 white mushrooms, thinly sliced

2 small onions, thinly sliced

3 cloves garlic, crushed and minced

2 celery stalks, cut into 1½-inch chunks

2 carrots, cut into 1½-inch chunks

¼ cup apple juice

2 bay leaves

¼ tsp. dried thyme

3–4 small Yukon gold potatoes, quartered

1 Tbsp. flour

½ cup frozen peas

1. Heat up your Instant Pot by pressing the Sauté button and click the adjust button to go to Sauté More function. Wait until the indicator says "hot."

2. Season one side of the chuck steak generously with salt and ground black pepper. Add olive oil into the inner pot. Be sure to coat the oil over whole bottom of the pot.

3. Carefully place the seasoned side of chuck steak in the inner pot. Generously season the other side with salt and ground black pepper. Brown for 6–8 minutes on each side without constantly flipping the steak. Remove and set aside in a large mixing bowl.

4. While the chuck steak is browning, mix together the Worcestershire sauce, light soy sauce, and tomato paste with the chicken stock.

5. Add sliced mushrooms into the Instant Pot. Sauté until all moisture from the mushrooms has evaporated and the edges are slightly crisped and browned, about 6 minutes. Taste and season with salt and ground black pepper if necessary. Remove and set aside.

6. Add olive oil into Instant Pot if necessary. Add thinly sliced small onions and sauté until softened and slightly browned. Add minced garlic cloves and stir for roughly 30 seconds until fragrant.

7. Add all celery and carrots and sauté until slightly browned. Season with salt and freshly ground black pepper if necessary.

8. Pour in apple juice and completely deglaze bottom of the pot by scrubbing the flavorful brown bits with a wooden spoon.

9. Add 2 bay leaves, dried thyme, quartered potatoes, and chicken stock mixture in the pot. Mix well. Close and secure lid and pressure cook on Manual at high pressure for 4 minutes. When time is up, quick release the pressure. Open the lid.

10. While the vegetables are pressure cooking, cut the chuck steak into 1½–2-inch stew cubes on a large chopping board.

11. Place all chuck stew meat and the flavorful meat juice back in the large mixing bowl. Add flour in mixing bowl and mix well with the stew meat.

12. Remove half of the carrots, celery, and potatoes from pressure cooker and set aside. Place beef stew meat and all its juice in the inner pot. Partially submerge the beef stew meat in the liquid without stirring, as you don't want too much flour in the liquid at this point.

13. Close and secure the lid and pressure cook on Manual at high pressure for 32 minutes. When time is up, turn off the Instant Pot and quick release any remaining pressure.

14. On medium heat by pressing the Sauté button, break down the mushy potatoes and carrots with a wooden spoon. Stir to thicken the stew.

15. Add frozen peas, sautéed mushrooms, and the set-aside carrots, celery, and potatoes in the pot. Taste and season with salt and ground black pepper if necessary.

16. Serve with mashed potatoes, pasta, or your favorite starch. Enjoy!

Beef and Kale Stew

Makes 6 servings

Dora Martindale, Elk City, OK

Prep. Time: 20 minutes 　⚘　 Cooking Time: 10 minutes 　⚘　 Setting: Sauté and Manual
Pressure: High 　⚘　 Release: Manual then Natural

1 cup sliced mushrooms

3 Tbsp. butter

2 lbs. ground beef

4 pieces nitrate-free bacon, chopped

2 bundles kale, finely chopped

4 cloves garlic, minced

2 onions, chopped

3–4 cups homemade
beef bone broth, divided

3 large potatoes, chopped

3 tsp. salt (or more to taste)

1 tsp. pepper (or more to taste)

2 Tbsp. dried thyme or 2 drops Young
Living Thyme Vitality Essential Oil

2 heaping tsp. non-GMO organic
cornstarch

1. In the inner pot of the Instant Pot, sauté mushrooms in the butter using the Sauté function, then place in a bowl.

2. Add the beef, chopped bacon, kale, garlic, and onions, and sauté until beef is brown and kale is reduced in size.

3. Add 2 cups bone broth, thyme, salt, and pepper. Secure the lid and make sure vent is at sealing, then cook on Manual at high pressure for 8 minutes.

4. Do a quick release of the pressure.

5. Add the rest of ingredients (except the cornstarch) and 1–2 more cups of bone broth.

6. Secure the lid and make sure vent is at sealing, then cook on Manual at high pressure 6 minutes. Let the pressure release naturally.

7. Thicken slightly with the cornstarch and add more salt or pepper as needed.

Favorite memory of sharing this recipe:
It's a healing recipe that is also delicious!

NOTE
from the cook

• I also make a chicken version of this and use butternut squash or sweet potatoes in place of the potatoes. Cut cooking time in half on second cook because these veggies take less time to cook.

• You can add just about any veggies to this.

White Chicken Chili

Makes 6 servings

Judy Gascho, Woodburn, OR

Prep. Time: 20 minutes ⚶ Cooking Time: 30 minutes ⚶ Setting: Bean/Chili
Pressure: High ⚶ Release: Natural then Manual

2 Tbsp. cooking oil

1½–2 lbs. boneless chicken breasts or thighs

1 medium onion, chopped

3 cloves garlic, minced

2 cups chicken broth

3 15-oz. cans great northern beans, undrained

15-oz. can white corn, drained

4½-oz. can chopped green chilies, undrained

1 tsp. cumin

½ tsp. ground oregano

1 cup sour cream

1½ cups grated cheddar or Mexican blend cheese

1. Set Instant Pot to Sauté and allow the inner pot to get hot.

2. Add oil and chicken. Brown chicken on both sides.

3. Add onions, garlic, chicken broth, undrained beans, drained corn, undrained green chilies, cumin, and oregano.

4. Place lid on and close valve to sealing.

5. Set to Bean/Chili for 30 minutes.

6. Let pressure release naturally for 15 minutes before carefully releasing any remaining steam.

7. Remove chicken and shred.

8. Put chicken, sour cream, and cheese in the inner pot. Stir until cheese is melted.

Serving suggestion:
Can serve with chopped cilantro and additional cheese.

Favorite Chili

Makes 4–6 servings

Carol Eveleth, Cheyenne, WY

Prep. Time: 10 minutes ⚬ *Cooking Time: 35 minutes* ⚬ *Setting: Manual*
Pressure: High ⚬ *Release: Natural*

I lb. ground beef

I tsp. salt

½ tsp. black pepper

I Tbsp. olive oil

I small onion, chopped

2 cloves garlic, minced

I green pepper, chopped

2 Tbsp. chili powder

½ tsp. cumin

I cup water

16-oz. can chili beans

15-oz. can crushed tomatoes

1. Press Sauté button and adjust once to Sauté More function. Wait until indicator says "hot."

2. Season the ground beef with salt and black pepper.

3. Add the olive oil into the inner pot. Coat the whole bottom of the pot with the oil.

4. Add ground beef into the inner pot. The ground beef will start to release moisture. Allow the ground beef to brown and crisp slightly, stirring occasionally to break it up. Taste and adjust the seasoning with more salt and ground black pepper.

5. Add diced onion, minced garlic, chopped pepper, chili powder, and cumin. Sauté for about 5 minutes, until the spices start to release their fragrance. Stir frequently.

6. Add water and can of chili beans, not drained. Mix well. Pour in can of crushed tomatoes.

7. Close and secure lid, making sure vent is set to sealing, and pressure cook on Manual at high pressure for 10 minutes.

8. Let the pressure release naturally when cooking time is up. Open the lid carefully.

Serving suggesiton:

Garnish chili with sour cream, shredded cheese, jalepeño slices, or chopped onions.

Serve over your favorite side dishes.

Potato and Corn Chowder

Makes 4–6 servings

Janie Steele, Moore, OK

Prep. Time: 10 minutes ⚓ *Cooking Time: 10 minutes* ⚓ *Setting: Sauté and Manual*
Pressure: High ⚓ *Release: Natural*

3 Tbsp. butter

¼ cup diced onion

6 medium red potatoes, diced

4 ears corn, or frozen or canned equal to 2 cups

3 cups vegetable broth or water

2 tsp. cornstarch

3 cups half-and-half

grated cheddar cheese, *optional*

1. Place the butter in the inner pot of the Instant Pot. Press the Sauté function and let the butter melt.

2. Sauté the onion in the butter until translucent.

3. Add the potatoes, corn, and 3 cups broth or water to the Inner Pot.

4. Secure the lid and set vent to sealing, then cook on Manual, high pressure, for 10 minutes.

5. Let the pressure release naturally, then remove lid.

6. Mix cornstarch in small amount of water and mix into soup to thicken.

7. With Instant Pot on sauté, add the half-and-half slowly while stirring.

8. Serve with cheddar cheese on top, if desired.

Main Dishes

Quick Steak Tacos

Makes 6 servings

Hope Comerford, Clinton Township, MI

Prep. Time: 5 minutes   ❧   *Cooking Time: 10 minutes*   ❧   *Setting: Sauté*

1 Tbsp. olive oil
8 oz. sirloin steak
2 Tbsp. steak seasoning
1 tsp. Worcestershire sauce
½ red onion, sliced
6 corn tortillas
¼ cup tomatoes
¾ cup reduced-fat Mexican cheese
2 Tbsp. sour cream
6 Tbsp. garden fresh salsa
¼ cup chopped fresh cilantro

1. Turn the Instant Pot on the Sauté function. When the pot displays "hot," add the olive oil to the pot.

2. Season the steak with the steak seasoning.

3. Add the steak to the pot along with the Worcestershire sauce.

4. Cook each side of the steak for 2–3 minutes until the steak turns brown.

5. Remove the steak from the pot and slice thinly.

6. Add the onion to the pot and cook them until translucent with the remaining olive oil and steak juices.

7. Remove the onion from the pot.

8. Warm your corn tortillas, then assemble your steak, onion, tomatoes, cheese, sour cream, salsa, and cilantro on top of each.

Pot Roast

Makes 4 servings

Carol Eveleth, Cheyenne, WY

Prep. Time: 20 min ⚶ *Cooking Time: 2 hours* ⚶ *Setting: Manual*
Pressure: High ⚶ *Release: Manual*

2 lbs. beef roast, boneless

¼ tsp. salt

¼ tsp. pepper

1 Tbsp. olive oil

2 stalks celery, chopped

4 Tbsp. butter

2 cups tomato juice

2 cloves garlic, finely chopped, or 1 tsp. garlic powder

1 tsp. thyme

1 bay leaf

4 carrots, chopped

1 medium onion, chopped

4 medium potatoes, chopped

Serving Suggestion:

Serve with a side of steamed broccoli to add some bright color to the dish!

1. Pat beef dry with paper towels; season on all sides with ¼ teaspoon each salt and pepper.

2. Select Sauté function on the Instant Pot and adjust heat to "more." Put the oil in the inner pot, then cook the beef in oil for 6 minutes, until browned, turning once. Set on plate.

3. Add celery and butter to the inner pot; cook 2 minutes. Stir in tomato juice, garlic, thyme, and bay leaf. Hit Cancel to turn off Sauté function.

4. Place beef on top of the contents of the inner pot and press into sauce. Cover and lock lid and make sure vent is at sealing. Select Manual and cook at high pressure for 1 hour 15 minutes.

5. Once cooking is complete, release pressure by using natural release function. Transfer beef to cutting board. Discard bay leaf.

6. Skim off any excess fat from surface. Choose Sauté function and adjust heat to "more." Cook 18 minutes, or until reduced by about half (2½ cups). Hit Cancel to turn off Sauté function.

7. Add carrots, onion, and potatoes. Cover and lock lid and make sure vent is at sealing. Select Manual and cook at high pressure for 10 minutes.

8. Once cooking is complete, release pressure by using a quick release. Using Sauté function, keep at a simmer.

9. Season with more salt and pepper to taste.

Beef Broccoli

Makes 6 servings

Anita Troyer, Fairview, MI

Prep. Time: 15 minutes ⚜ *Cooking Time: 20 minutes* ⚜ *Setting: Manual and Sauté*
Pressure: High ⚜ *Release: Manual*

1 Tbsp. oil

1 ½ lbs. boneless beef, trimmed and sliced thinly (round steak or chuck roast)

¼ tsp. black pepper

½ cup diced onion

3 cloves garlic, minced

¾ cup beef broth

½ cup soy sauce

¼ cup brown sugar

2 Tbsp. sesame oil

¼ tsp. red pepper flakes

1 lb. broccoli, chopped

3 Tbsp. water

3 Tbsp. cornstarch

1. Put oil into the inner pot of the Instant Pot and select Sauté. When oil begins to sizzle, brown the beef in several small batches, taking care to brown well. After browning, remove and put into another bowl. Season with black pepper.

2. Sauté onion in pot for 2 minutes. Add garlic and sauté another minute. Add beef broth, soy sauce, brown sugar, sesame oil, and red pepper flakes. Stir to mix well. Add beef and juices on it.

3. Add beef to mixture in inner pot. Secure lid and make sure vent is at sealing. Set on Manual at high pressure and set timer for 12 minutes.

4. After beep, turn cooker off and use quick pressure release. Remove lid.

5. In microwave bowl, steam the broccoli for 3 minutes or until desired doneness.

6. In a small bowl, stir together water and cornstarch. Add to pot and stir. Put on Sauté setting and stir some more. After mixture becomes thick, add broccoli and turn pot off.

Serving suggestion:
Serve over rice.

Philly Cheese Steaks

Makes 6 servings

Michele Ruvola, Vestal, NY

Prep. Time: 15 minutes ⚜ *Cooking Time: 55 minutes* ⚜ *Setting: Slow Cook*
Pressure: Low ⚜ *Release: Natural then Manual*

1 red pepper, sliced
1 green pepper, sliced
1 onion, sliced
2 cloves garlic, minced
2½ lbs. thinly sliced steak
1 tsp. salt
½ tsp. black pepper
0.7-oz. pkg. dry Italian dressing mix
1 cup water
1 beef bouillon cube
6 slices of provolone cheese
6 hoagie rolls

1. Put all ingredients in the inner pot of the Instant Pot, except the provolone cheese and rolls.

2. Seal the lid, make sure vent is at sealing, and cook for 40 minutes on the Slow Cook setting.

3. Let the pressure release naturally for 10 minutes, then do a quick release.

4. Scoop meat and vegetables into rolls.

5. Top with provolone cheese and put on a baking sheet.

6. Broil in oven for 5 minutes.

7. Pour remaining juice in pot into cups for dipping.

Bell Pepper Casserole

Makes 6 servings

Janie Steele, Moore, OK

Prep. Time: 10 minutes ⚭ *Cooking Time: 10 minutes* ⚭ *Setting: Manual*
Pressure: High ⚭ *Release: Natural*

1 lb. ground beef

1 Tbsp. olive oil

¾ cup long-grain rice

3–4 bell peppers, diced (your choice of colors)

½ cup diced onions

6-oz. can diced chilies

14-oz. can diced tomatoes

24-oz. jar Ragú or Prego brand marinara sauce

½ tsp. chili powder

1 tsp. seasoned salt

2–3 cloves garlic, minced

1. Using the Sauté function, sauté the beef in the olive oil in inner pot of the Instant Pot.

2. Add in the peppers and onions, then turn the Instant Pot off by hitting the Cancel button.

3. Add the remaining ingredients. Do NOT stir.

4. Secure the lid and make sure vent is at sealing. Turn the Instant Pot on Manual for 10 minutes.

5. Let the pressure release naturally.

Serving suggestion:

Serve with cheese: mozzarella, or Parmesan.

Pork Butt Roast

Makes 6–8 servings

Marla Folkerts, Batavia, IL

Prep. Time: 10 minutes ⚘ *Cooking Time: 9 minutes* ⚘ *Setting: Manual*
Pressure: High ⚘ *Release: Natural*

3–4-lb. pork butt roast
2–3 Tbsp. of your favorite rub
2 cups water

1. Place pork in the inner pot of the Instant Pot.

2. Sprinkle in the rub all over the roast and add the water, being careful not to wash off the rub.

3. Secure the lid and set the vent to sealing. Cook for 9 minutes on the Manual setting.

4. Let the pressure release naturally.

Pulled Pork

Makes 8 servings

Colleen Heatwole, Burton, MI

Prep. Time: 15 minutes ❧ Cooking Time: 75 minutes ❧ Setting: Meat/Stew
Pressure: High ❧ Release: Natural

2 Tbsp. vegetable oil

4-lb. boneless pork shoulder, cut into two pieces

2 cups barbecue sauce, *divided*

½ cup water

1. Add oil to the inner pot of the Instant Pot and select Sauté.

2. When oil is hot, brown pork on both sides, about 3 minutes per side. Brown each half of roast separately. Remove to platter when browned.

3. Add 1 cup barbecue sauce and ½ cup water to the inner pot. Stir to combine.

4. Add browned pork and any accumulated juices to the inner pot. Secure the lid and set vent to sealing.

5. Using Meat/Stew mode, set timer to 60 minutes, on high pressure.

6. When cook time is up, allow the pressure to release naturally.

7. Carefully remove meat and shred with two forks, discarding excess fat as you shred.

8. Strain cooking liquid, reserving ½ cup. If possible use fat separator to separate fat from juices.

9. Place shredded pork in the inner pot with with remaining 1 cup barbecue sauce and reserved ½ cup cooking liquid. Using Sauté function, stir to combine and bring to a simmer, stirring frequently.

NOTE

from the cook

Pork shoulder releases a lot of fat and juices, making meat flavorful and tender. However, using a fat separator helps to reduce fat on final product.

Serving suggestion:

We serve on toasted buns. Our barbecue sauce of choice is Sweet Baby Ray's.

BBQ Pork Sandwiches

Makes 4 servings

Carol Eveleth, Cheyenne, WY

Prep. Time: 20 minutes ⚜ *Cooking Time: 1 hour* ⚜ *Setting: Manual and Sauté*
Pressure: High ⚜ *Release: Manual*

2 tsp. salt

I tsp. onion powder

I tsp. garlic powder

2-lb. pork shoulder roast, cut into
3-inch pieces

I Tbsp. olive oil

2 cups barbecue sauce

1. In a small bowl, combine the salt, onion powder, and garlic powder. Season the pork with the rub.

2. Turn the Instant Pot on to Sauté. Heat the olive oil in the inner pot.

3. Add the pork to the oil and turn to coat. Lock the lid and set vent to sealing.

4. Press Manual and cook on high pressure for 45 minutes.

5. When cooking is complete, realease the pressure manually, then open the lid.

6. Using 2 forks, shred the pork, pour barbecue sauce over the pork, then press Sauté. Simmer, 3 to 5 minutes. Press Cancel. Toss pork to mix.

Serving suggestion:

Pile the shredded BBQ pork on the bottom half of a bun. Add any additional toppings if you wish, then finish with the top half of the bun.

Philippine Ulam

Makes 4–6 servings

Carol Eveleth, Cheyenne, WY

Prep. Time: 25 minutes ⚬ *Cooking Time: 30 minutes* ⚬ *Setting: Manual*
Pressure: High ⚬ *Release: Natural then Manual*

2 lbs. cubed pork chunks
¼ tsp. black pepper
1–2 Tbsp. oil
4 cups cubed potatoes
3 bell peppers, diced
¼ cup lemon juice
½ cup soy sauce
4 cups water

1. Sprinkle pork chunks with pepper.

2. Press Sauté. When the word "hot" appears, swirl in oil in the inner pot.

3. Place the cubed pork chunks in the inner pot and cook 5 minutes, or until golden brown on all sides.

4. Add cubed potatoes, peppers, lemon juice, soy sauce, and water.

5. Close and lock the lid of the Instant Pot. Turn the steam release handle to sealing position. Cook on Manual at high pressure for 20 minutes. Allow a 10-minute natural pressure release. Turn steam release handle to venting to release remaining pressure.

Serving suggesiton:
Serve over cooked rice.

Tender Tasty Ribs

Makes 2–3 servings

Carol Eveleth, Cheyenne, WY

*Prep. Time: 5 minutes ♣ Cooking Time: 35 minutes ♣ Setting: Manual
Pressure: High ♣ Release: Natural*

2 tsp. salt

2 tsp. black pepper

I tsp. garlic powder

I tsp. onion powder

I slab baby back ribs

I cup water

I cup barbecue sauce, *divided*

1. Mix salt, pepper, garlic powder, and onion powder together. Rub seasoning mixture on both sides of slab of ribs. Cut slab in half if it's too big for your Instant Pot.

2. Pour water into inner pot of the Instant Pot. Place ribs into pot, drizzle with ¼ cup of sauce, and secure lid. Make sure the vent is set to sealing.

3. Set it to Manual for 25 minutes. It will take a few minutes to heat up and seal the vent. When cook time is up, let it sit 5 minutes, then release steam by turning valve to venting. Turn oven on to broil (or heat your grill) while you're waiting for the 5-minute resting time.

4. Remove ribs from Instant Pot and place on a baking sheet. Slather both sides with remaining ¾ cup sauce.

5. Place under broiler (or on grill) for 5–10 minutes, watching carefully so it doesn't burn. Remove and brush with a bit more sauce. Pull apart and dig in!

Pork Baby Back Ribs

Makes 6–8 servings

Marla Folkerts, Batavia, IL

Prep. Time: 20 minutes ⚶ *Cooking Time: 30 minutes* ⚶ *Setting: Meat*
Pressure: High ⚶ *Release: Natural then Manual*

3 racks of ribs
1 cup brown sugar
1 cup white sugar
1 tsp. garlic powder
1 tsp. garlic salt
1 cup of water
½ cup of apple cider vinegar
1 tsp. liquid smoke
½ cup barbecue sauce

1. Take the membrane/skin off the back of the ribs.

2. Mix together the remaining ingredients (except the barbecue sauce) and slather it on the ribs.

3. Place the ribs around the inside of the inner pot instead of stacking them. Secure the lid in place and make sure vent is at sealing.

4. Use the Meat setting and set for 30 minutes on high pressure.

5. When cooking time is up, let the pressure release naturally for 10 minutes, then do a quick release of the remaining pressure.

6. Place the ribs on a baking sheet and cover them with the barbecue sauce. Broil for 7–10 minutes (watching so they don't burn).

NOTE
from the cook
These were the best ribs I've ever had. They fell off the bone.

Instant Pot
TIP
I think placing the ribs around the pot instead of stacking makes it easier.

Teriyaki Ribs

Makes 2–3 servings

Janie Steele, Moore, OK

Prep. Time: 10 minutes ❧ *Cooking Time: 25 minutes* ❧ *Setting: Manual*
Pressure: High ❧ *Release: Natural*

½ Tbsp. chopped ginger

1 cup beef broth

½ cup soy sauce

1 Tbsp. minced garlic

4 Tbsp. brown sugar

2 Tbsp. sriracha sauce, or more to taste

⅓ cup hoisin sauce

1 rack ribs (1–2 lbs.)

1. Mix all ingredients together in a bowl, except the ribs.

2. Cut ribs into smaller 2–3 rib sections and place in bottom of the inner pot of the Instant Pot.

3. Pour the sauce on top.

4. Secure the lid and make sure vent is at sealing. Set to Manual and cook on high pressure for 25 minutes.

5. Let the pressure release naturally.

6. Serve as is, or if you want crispier coating, set oven to 375°F and bake for about 5 minutes.

7. Reserve sauce from pot as desired for extra moisture.

Garlic Galore Rotisserie Chicken

Makes 4 servings

Hope Comerford, Clinton Township, MI

Prep. Time: 5 minutes ⚜ *Cooking Time: 33 minutes* ⚜ *Setting: Sauté and Manual*
Pressure: High ⚜ *Release: Natural then Manual*

3-lb. whole chicken

2 Tbsp. olive oil, *divided*

salt to taste

pepper to taste

20–30 cloves fresh garlic, peeled and left whole

1 cup chicken stock, broth, or water

2 Tbsp. garlic powder

2 tsp. onion powder

½ tsp. basil

½ tsp. cumin

½ tsp. chili powder

1. Rub chicken with one tablespoon of the olive oil and sprinkle with salt and pepper.

2. Place the garlic cloves inside the chicken. Use butcher's twine to secure the legs.

3. Press the Sauté button on the Instant Pot then add the rest of the olive oil to the inner pot.

4. When the pot is hot, place the chicken inside. You are just trying to sear it, so leave it for about 4 minutes on each side.

5. Remove the chicken and set aside. Place the trivet at the bottom of the inner pot and pour in the chicken stock.

6. Mix together the remaining seasonings and rub it all over the entire chicken.

7. Place the chicken back inside the inner pot, breast side up, on top of the trivet and secure the lid to the sealing position.

8. Press the Manual button and use the +/- to set it for 25 minutes.

9. When the timer beeps, allow the pressure to release naturally for 15 minutes. If the lid will not open at this point, quick release the remaining pressure and remove the chicken.

10. Let the chicken rest for 5–10 minutes before serving.

Butter Chicken

Makes 4 servings

Jessica Stoner, Arlington, OH

Prep. Time: 10–15 minutes ♨ *Cooking Time: 20 minutes* ♨ *Setting: Sauté and Poultry*
Pressure: High ♨ *Release: Manual*

1 Tbsp. olive oil

1 medium onion, diced

1–2 medium cloves garlic, minced

½ Tbsp. minced ginger

1 tsp. garam masala

½ tsp. turmeric

2 tsp. kosher salt

2 lbs. cubed boneless skinless chicken breast

¼ cup tomato paste

2 cups crushed tomatoes

½ cup water

1½ Tbsp. honey

1½ cups heavy cream

1 Tbsp. butter

1. On Sauté function at high heat, heat oil in the inner pot of the Instant Pot. Add onion, garlic, and ginger and sauté for 1 minute, until fragrant and onion is soft.

2. Add garam masala, turmeric, and salt. Sauté quickly and add chicken. Stir to coat chicken. Add tomato paste and crushed tomatoes. Slowly add water, scraping the bottom of the pot with a spoon to make sure there are no bits of tomato stuck to the bottom. Stir in honey.

3. Secure the lid, making sure vent is turned to sealing function. Use the Poultry high pressure function and set cook time to 15 minutes. Once done cooking, do a quick release of the pressure.

4. Remove lid and change to medium/normal Sauté function and stir in heavy cream and bring to a simmer. Simmer for 5 minutes, adding up to ¼ cup additional water if you need to thin the sauce out. Stir in butter until melted and turn off.

Serving suggestion:
Serve hot with basmati rice and naan bread.

Buttery Lemon Chicken

Makes 4 servings

Judy Gascho, Woodburn, OR

Prep. Time: 15 minutes ⚜ Cooking Time: 7 minutes ⚜ Setting: Poultry
Pressure: High ⚜ Release: Natural

2 Tbsp. butter

1 medium onion, chopped

4 cloves garlic, minced

½ tsp. paprika

½ tsp. pepper

1 tsp. dried parsley, or 1 Tbsp. chopped fresh parsley

2 lbs. boneless chicken breasts or thighs

½ cup chicken broth

⅓ cup lemon juice

1 tsp. salt

1–2 Tbsp. cornstarch

1 Tbsp. water

1. Set the Instant Pot to Sauté. When it is hot, add butter to the inner pot and melt.

2. Add the onion, garlic, paprika, pepper, and parsley to melted butter and sauté until onion starts to soften. Push onion to side of pot.

3. With the Instant Pot still at sauté, add the chicken and sear on each side 3–5 minutes.

4. Mix broth, lemon juice, and salt together. Pour over chicken and stir to mix all together.

5. Put on lid and set Instant Pot, move vent to sealing and press Poultry. Set cook time for 7 minutes. Let depressurize naturally.

6. Remove chicken, leaving sauce in pot. Mix cornstarch in water and add to sauce. (Can start with 1 Tbsp. cornstarch, and use second one if sauce isn't thick enough.)

Serving suggestion:

Serve chicken and sauce over noodles or rice.

Chicken with Lemon

Makes 4 servings

Colleen Heatwole, Burton, MI

Prep. Time: 15 minutes ❧ *Cooking Time: 8 minutes* ❧ *Setting: Manual*
Pressure: High ❧ *Release: Natural*

2 lbs. boneless skinless chicken thighs

3 Tbsp. olive oil, *divided*

1 tsp. rosemary

1 tsp. kosher salt

½ tsp. black pepper

1 lemon, organic preferred

1 medium onion, diced

2 cloves garlic, minced

2 Tbsp. water

1. Toss chicken with 1 Tbsp. oil, rosemary, salt, and pepper.

2. Wash lemon, trim ends, quarter lengthwise, and remove seeds. Slice quarters crosswise into ⅛-inch slices.

3. Heat remaining 2 Tbsp. oil in the inner pot using Sauté function of the Instant Pot.

4. Add onion and garlic and sauté 3 minutes, stirring frequently.

5. Add lemon and sauté an additional minute.

6. Add the 2 Tbsp. water.

7. Add chicken and stir to combine.

8. Secure the lid and set vent to sealing. Cook 8 minutes, using Manual at high pressure.

9. Allow pressure to release naturally.

Favorite memory of sharing this recipe:
My husband loves this lemon chicken recipe. It is one I adapted from a conventional recipe because we like chicken with lemon.

Slow Cooked Honey Garlic Chicken Thighs

Makes 2–4 servings

Colleen Heatwole, Burton, MI

Prep. Time: 10 minutes ⚭ *Cooking Time: 4 hours* ⚭ *Setting: Slow Cook* ⚭ *Pressure: Low*

4 boneless skinless chicken thighs

2 Tbsp. soy sauce

½ cup ketchup

⅓ cup honey

3 cloves garlic, minced

1 tsp. basil

1. Place chicken thighs in bottom of the inner pot of the Instant Pot.

2. Whisk remaining ingredients together in bowl and pour over chicken.

3. Cook covered on the Slow Cook function on low pressure for 4 hours. Check for doneness. If not tender add additional time as needed.

Favorite memory of sharing this recipe:

This is a hit with children and adults.

NOTE

from the cook

Of course this can be done in a conventional slow cooker as well.

Instant Pot

TIP

I use a glass lid that is designed for a larger skillet, and it works well if you have not purchased the glass lid that fits the Instant Pot.

Lemony Chicken Thighs

Makes 3–5 servings

Maria Shevlin, Sicklerville, NJ

Prep. Time: 15 minutes ⚬ Cooking Time: 15 minutes ⚬ Setting: Poultry
Pressure: High ⚬ Release: Natural then Manual

I cup chicken bone broth

5 frozen bone-in chicken thighs

I small onion, diced

5–6 cloves garlic, diced

juice of I lemon

2 Tbsp. butter, melted

½ tsp. salt

¼ tsp. black pepper

I tsp. True Lemon Lemon Pepper seasoning

I tsp. parsley flakes

¼ tsp. oregano

rind of I lemon

1. Add the chicken bone broth into the inner pot of the Instant Pot.

2. Add the chicken thighs.

3. Add the onion and garlic.

4. Pour the fresh lemon juice in with the melted butter.

5. Add the seasonings.

6. Lock the lid, make sure the vent is at sealing, then press the Poultry button. Set to 15 minutes.

7. When cook time is up, let the pressure naturally release for 3–5 minutes, then manually release the rest.

8. You can place these under the broiler for 2–3 minutes to brown.

9. Plate up and pour some of the sauce over top with fresh grated lemon rind.

Orange Chicken Breasts

Makes 6 servings

Anita Troyer, Fairview, MI

Prep. Time: 20 minutes ⚘ *Cooking Time: 15 minutes* ⚘ *Setting: Sauté and Manual*
Pressure: High ⚘ *Release: Manual*

2 lbs. chicken breasts
2 Tbsp. oil

Sauce:

1 cup orange juice
1 Tbsp. grated fresh ginger
4 cloves garlic, minced
1 Tbsp. rice wine
½ cup tomato sauce
⅓ cup brown sugar
¼ cup soy sauce
zest from an orange

2 Tbsp. orange juice
2 Tbsp. cornstarch

1. Cut the chicken into 1–2-inch pieces.

2. Turn Instant Pot to Sauté. Once hot, add the oil to the inner pot. After the oil is hot, add the chicken and fry for 2–3 minutes, stirring several times. Make sure the chicken doesn't stick to the bottom of the pot.

3. Add the sauce ingredients to the chicken in the pot and stir to combine and coat chicken well.

4. Secure the lid on the pot and make sure vent is at sealing. Press the Manual function, at high pressure, for 5 minutes.

5. When cook time is up, turn off the Instant Pot and manually release the pressure.

6. Remove lid and turn pot on to Sauté.

7. Combine the orange juice and cornstarch in a small bowl and stir until well mixed. Add to pot and gently stir to combine. If stirred too vigorously, the chicken will fall apart.

8. Keep on Sauté setting until thickened, 2–3 minutes. Turn pot off.

Serving suggestion:
Serve over rice.

NOTE
from the cook
This is even better in leftovers as the meat has time to flavor.

Orange Chicken Thighs with Bell Peppers

Makes 4–6 servings

Maria Shevlin, Sicklerville, NJ

Prep. Time: 15–20 minutes & Cooking Time: 7 minutes & Setting: Sauté and Manual
Pressure: High & Release: Manual

6 boneless skinless chicken thighs, cut into bite-size pieces

2 packets crystallized True Orange flavoring

½ tsp. True Orange Orange Ginger seasoning

½ tsp. coconut aminos

¼ tsp. Worcestershire sauce

olive oil or cooking spray

2 cups bell pepper strips, any color combination (I used red, yellow, and orange)

1 onion, chopped

1 Tbsp. green onion, chopped fine

3 cloves garlic, minced or chopped

½ tsp. pink salt

½ tsp. black pepper

1 tsp. garlic powder

1 tsp. ground ginger

¼–½ tsp. red pepper flakes

2 Tbsp. tomato paste

½ cup chicken bone broth or water

1 Tbsp. brown sugar substitute (I use Sukrin Gold)

½ cup Seville orange spread (I use Crofter's brand)

1. Combine the chicken with the 2 packets of crystallized orange flavor, the orange ginger seasoning, the coconut aminos, and the Worcestershire sauce. Set aside.

2. Turn the Instant Pot to Sauté and add a touch of olive oil or cooking spray to the inner pot. Add in the orange ginger marinated chicken thighs.

3. Sauté until lightly browned. Add in the peppers, onions, garlic, and seasonings. Mix well.

4. Add the remaining ingredients; mix to combine.

5. Lock the lid, set the vent to sealing, set to 7 minutes.

6. Let the pressure release naturally for 2 minutes, then manually release the rest when cook time is up.

NOTE
from the cook

• The sauce will be on the thinner side, so if you don't care for a thin sauce, use a thickener of your choice. You can put the pot back on to sauté and stir till thickened.

• I love to use True Lemon and True Orange products because they are natural, good for you, and each purchase goes to a good cause.

Serving suggestion:

Serve with your choice of pasta or rice and top with additional green onion and/or sesame seeds as well.

Insta Pasta à la Maria

Makes 6–8 servings

Maria Shevlin, Sicklerville, NJ

Prep. Time: 10–15 minutes ❦ *Cooking Time: 6 minutes* ❦ *Setting: Manual*
Pressure: High ❦ *Release: Manual*

32-oz. jar of your favorite spaghetti sauce or 1 quart of homemade

2 cups fresh chopped spinach

1 cup chopped mushrooms

½ precooked whole rotisserie chicken, shredded

1 tsp. salt

½ tsp. black pepper

½ tsp. dried basil

¼ tsp. red pepper flakes

1 tsp. parsley flakes

13¼-oz. box pasta, any shape or brand (I used Dreamfield)

3 cups water

1. Place the sauce in the bottom of the inner pot of the Instant Pot.

2. Add in the spinach, then the mushrooms.

3. Add the chicken on top of the veggies and sauce.

4. Add the seasonings and give it a stir to mix.

5. Add the box of pasta.

6. Add 3 cups of water.

7. Secure the lid and move vent to sealing. Set to Manual on high pressure for 6 minutes.

8. When cook time is up, release the pressure manually.

9. Remove the lid and stir to mix together.

Thai Chicken and Noodles

Makes 4 servings

Vonnie Oyer, Hubbard, OR

Prep. Time: 15 minutes ⚘ *Cooking Time: 30 minutes* ⚘ *Setting: Manual then Slow Cook*
Pressure: High ⚘ *Release: Manual*

Thai peanut sauce:

¾ cup light coconut milk

½ cup peanut butter

2 Tbsp. sesame oil

¼ cup fresh lime juice

2 Tbsp. soy sauce

1½ tsp. crushed red pepper flakes

1 Tbsp. seasoned rice vinegar

1 Tbsp. honey

¼ tsp. ground ginger

1½ lbs. boneless skinless chicken breasts

1½ cups chicken broth

8 oz. dry rice noodles

5 oz. sugar snap peas (about 1½ cups)

1. Mix all the sauce ingredients in a blender. Makes 2 cups (this recipe uses 1 cup).

2. To the inner pot of the Instant Pot, add the chicken, 1 cup Thai peanut sauce, and broth.

3. Secure the lid and make sure vent is at sealing. Cook on Manual at high pressure for 12 minutes.

4. Do a quick release (manual) of the pressure. Remove the chicken from pot, leaving the sauce.

5. To the sauce, add the noodles and ensure all of the dry noodles are submerged in sauce. Top with the peas and replace the cover as quickly as possible.

6. Change the setting to Slow Cook and cook for 10 minutes, or until the noodles are soft but firm.

7. Meanwhile, shred the chicken breasts and set aside.

8. When cook time is up, remove the lid of the Instant Pot and give the noodles a good stir. Stir the chicken back into the inner pot with the noodles.

Thai Chicken Rice Bowls

Makes 4–6 servings

Vonnie Oyer, Hubbard, OR

Prep. Time: 15 minutes ❧ *Cooking Time: 20 minutes* ❧ *Setting: Sauté and Manual*
Pressure: High ❧ *Release: Natural*

2 Tbsp. olive oil

2 lbs. chicken breasts (about 4)

½ cup sweet chili Thai sauce

3 Tbsp. soy sauce

½ Tbsp. fish sauce

½ Tbsp. minced ginger

½ Tbsp. minced garlic

1 tsp. lime juice

1 tsp. sriracha sauce

1 Tbsp. peanut butter

1 cup uncooked long-grain white rice

2 cups broth

Optional garnishes:

cilantro
shredded carrots
peanuts

1. Select the Sauté setting on the Instant Pot and add the olive oil to the inner pot.

2. Sear the chicken for 2–3 minutes on both sides to seal in their juices. Remove to a glass baking dish and turn off the Instant Pot.

3. Mix the sweet chili Thai sauce, soy sauce, fish sauce, ginger, garlic, lime juice, sriracha, and peanut butter together.

4. Pour the sauce over the chicken breasts in glass dish.

5. Place the rice in the inner pot of the Instant Pot and add the chicken and sauce over top.

6. Add the broth and secure the lid. Make sure vent is on sealing.

7. Select the Manual setting (on high pressure) and set the timer to 10 minutes. Let pressure release naturally.

8. Take out and shred the chicken with two forks. Mix the chicken back in with the rice.

9. Garnish with cilantro, shredded carrots, and peanuts, if desired.

Chicken Broccoli and Rice

Makes 4 servings

Jessica Stoner, Arlington, OH

Prep. Time: 15–20 minutes ⚓ *Cooking Time: 5 minutes* ⚓ *Setting: Sauté and Manual*
Pressure: High ⚓ *Release: Manual*

2 Tbsp. butter

1½–2 lbs. boneless skinless chicken breast, cut into cubes

2 cloves garlic

1 small onion, chopped

1⅓ cups long-grain rice

1⅓ cups chicken broth

1 tsp. salt

¾ tsp. pepper

1 tsp. garlic powder

½ cup milk

1½ Tbsp. flour

1–2 cups fresh broccoli, cooked

1½–2 cups shredded mild cheddar cheese

1. Turn Instant Pot to Sauté. Add butter to the inner pot and heat until hot. When hot add chicken, garlic, and onion.

2. Cook chicken mixture until onion starts to get translucent. Add rice, broth, and seasonings. Stir well.

3. Whisk together milk and flour and set aside.

4. Secure the lid and make sure vent is at sealing. Cook on Manual on high pressure for 5 minutes. When time is up perform a quick release.

5. Remove lid and immediately add milk and flour mixture and mix until it is well combined.

6. Add broccoli and cheese and stir until well combined. Serve immediately.

Chicken with Spiced Sesame Sauce

Makes 4–6 servings

Colleen Heatwole, Burton, MI

Prep. Time: 20 minutes & Cooking Time: 8 minutes & Setting: Manual
Pressure: High & Release: Manual

2 Tbsp. tahini (sesame sauce)

¼ cup water

1 Tbsp. soy sauce

¼ cup chopped onion

1 tsp. red wine vinegar

2 tsp. minced garlic

1 tsp. shredded ginger root (Microplane works best)

2 lbs. chicken breast, chopped into 8 portions

1. Place first seven ingredients in bottom of the inner pot of the Instant Pot.

2. Add coarsely chopped chicken on top.

3. Secure the lid and make sure vent is at sealing. Set for 8 minutes using Manual setting. When cook time is up, let the pressure release naturally for 10 minutes, then perform a quick release.

4. Remove ingredients and shred chicken with forks. Combine with other ingredients in pot for a tasty sandwich filling or sauce.

NOTE
from the cook

This is a recipe I liked that I adapted to the Instant Pot.

Mild Chicken Curry with Coconut Milk

Makes 4–6 servings

Brittney Horst, Lititz, PA

Prep. Time: 10 minutes ⚜ *Cooking Time: 14 minutes* ⚜ *Setting: Sauté and Manual*
Pressure: High ⚜ *Release: Natural*

1 large onion, diced

6 cloves garlic, crushed

¼ cup coconut oil (butter or avocado oil would work fine, too)

½ tsp. black pepper

½ tsp. turmeric

½ tsp. paprika

¼ tsp. cinnamon

¼ tsp. cloves

¼ tsp. cumin

¼ tsp. ginger

½ tsp. salt

1 Tbsp. curry powder (more if you like more flavor)

½ tsp. chili powder

24-oz. can of diced or crushed tomatoes

13½-oz. can of coconut milk (I prefer a brand that has no unwanted ingredients, like guar gum or sugar)

4 lbs. boneless skinless chicken breasts, cut into chunks

1. Sauté onion and garlic in oil, either with Sauté setting in the inner pot of the Instant Pot, or on stove top and add to pot.

2. Combine spices in a small bowl, then add to the inner pot.

3. Add tomatoes and coconut milk and stir.

4. Add chicken, and stir to coat the pieces with the sauce.

5. Secure the lid and make sure vent is at sealing. Set to Manual mode (or Pressure Cook on newer models) for 14 minutes.

6. Let pressure release naturally (or, if you're crunched for time, you can do a quick release).

7. Serve with your favorite sides, and enjoy!

Serving suggestion:

We like it on rice, with a couple of veggies on the side.

Favorite memory of sharing this recipe:

My eleven-month-old ate this!!! No joke! So it's not too spicy for those who don't like their food too hot, but can be more flavorful if you want to add more spice.

Instant Pot TIP
On the newest Instant Pot, I do not like the Sauté feature. I find it too hot and food will burn.

Cheesy Stuffed Cabbage

Makes 6–8 servings

Maria Shevlin, Sicklerville, NJ

Prep. Time: 30 minutes ⚘ Cooking Time: 18 minutes ⚘ Setting: Manual
Pressure: High ⚘ Release: Manual

1–2 heads savoy cabbage
1 lb. ground turkey
1 egg
1 cup shredded cheddar cheese
2 Tbsp. heavy cream
¼ cup shredded Parmesan cheese
¼ cup shredded mozzarella cheese
¼ cup finely diced onion
¼ cup finely diced bell pepper
¼ cup finely diced mushrooms
1 tsp. salt
½ tsp. black pepper
1 tsp. garlic powder
6 basil leaves, fresh and cut chiffonade
1 Tbsp. fresh parsley, chopped
1 qt. of your favorite pasta sauce

1. Remove the core from the cabbages.

2. Boil water and place 1 head at a time into the water for approximately 10 minutes.

3. Allow cabbage to cool slightly. Once cooled, remove the leaves carefully and set aside. You'll need about 15 or 16.

4. Mix together the meat and all remaining ingredients except the pasta sauce.

5. One leaf at a time, put a heaping tablespoon of meat mixture in the center.

6. Tuck the sides in and then roll tightly.

7. Add ½ cup sauce to the bottom of the inner pot of the Instant Pot.

8. Place the rolls, fold side down, into the pot and layer them, putting a touch of sauce between each layer and finally on top. (You may want to cook the rolls half a batch at a time.)

9. Lock lid and make sure vent is at sealing. Set timer on 18 minutes on Manual at high pressure, then manually release the pressure when cook time is over.

Taylor's Favorite Uniquely Stuffed Peppers

Makes 4 servings

Maria Shevlin, Sicklerville, NJ

Prep. Time: 20–30 minutes ❧ Cooking Time: 15 minutes ❧ Setting: Manual
Pressure: High ❧ Release: Manual

4 red bell peppers
1 tsp. olive oil
½ onion, chopped
3 cloves garlic, minced
½ lb. ground turkey
½ lb. spicy Italian sausage
1 tsp. salt
½ tsp. black pepper
1 tsp. garlic powder
½ tsp. dried oregano
½ tsp. dried basil
1 medium zucchini, grated and water pressed out
½ cup of your favorite barbecue sauce
¼ cup quick oats
1 cup water or bone broth

1. Cut the stem part of the top off the bell peppers, remove seeds and membranes, and set aside.

2. Add olive oil, onion, and garlic to a pan. Cook till al dente.

3. Add in your ground turkey and sausage, and brown lightly.

4. Add in your seasonings, zucchini, and barbecue sauce.

5. Add in your oats.

6. Mix well to combine.

7. Stuff the filling inside each pepper—pack it in.

8. Add 1 cup of water or bone broth to the bottom of the inner pot of the Instant Pot.

9. Add the rack to the pot.

10. Arrange the stuffed peppers standing upright in the pot.

11. Lock lid, make sure vent is at sealing, and use the Manual setting to set for 15 minutes.

12. When cook time is up, release the pressure manually.

Favorite memory of sharing this recipe:

My daughter absolutely prefers this over any other way I make stuffed peppers.

Ground Turkey Cacciatore Spaghetti

Makes 6 servings

Maria Shevlin, Sicklerville, NJ

Prep. Time: 15–20 minutes ⚜ *Cooking Time: 5 minutes* ⚜ *Setting: Sauté and Manual*
Pressure: High ⚜ *Release: Manual*

I tsp. olive oil

I medium sweet onion, chopped

3 cloves garlic, minced

I lb. ground turkey

32-oz. jar spaghetti sauce, or I qt. homemade

I tsp. salt

½ tsp. black pepper

½ tsp. oregano

½ tsp. dried basil

½ tsp. red pepper flakes

I cup bell pepper strips, mixed colors if desired

I cup diced mushrooms

13¼-oz. box Dreamfield spaghetti

3 cups chicken bone broth

1. Press the Sauté button on the Instant Pot and add the oil, onion, and garlic to the inner pot.

2. Add in the ground turkey and break it up a little while it browns.

3. Once ground turkey is browned, add in the sauce and seasonings.

4. Add in the bell peppers and mushrooms and give it a stir to mix.

5. Add in the spaghetti—break it in half in order for it to fit in.

6. Add in the chicken bone broth.

7. Lock lid, make sure the vent is at sealing, and set on Manual at high pressure for 6 minutes.

8. When cook time is up, manually release the pressure.

Serving suggestion:
Top with some fresh grated Parmesan cheese and basil.

Daddy's Pasta Fasool

Makes 8 servings

Maria Shevlin, Sicklerville, NJ

Prep. Time: 15 minutes ⚘ Cooking Time: 6 minutes ⚘ Setting: Sauté and Manual
Pressure: High ⚘ Release: Manual

1 cup tomato sauce
1 cup diced onion
½ cup diced carrots
½ cup diced celery
1 Tbsp. chopped fresh celery leaves
14½-oz. can petite diced tomatoes
1 cup precooked ground turkey
3–4 cloves garlic, minced
1 bay leaf
½ tsp. onion powder
½ tsp. garlic powder
¼ tsp. basil
¼ tsp. oregano
½ tsp. parsley flakes
½ tsp. salt
¼ tsp. black pepper
15½-oz. can cannelini beans, drained and rinsed (I use Goya brand)
1 cup Dreamfield elbows or similar small pasta of your choice
4 cups chicken bone broth

1. In the inner pot of the Instant Pot, add the sauce, vegetables, tomatoes, meat, and seasonings, and stir.

2. Set to Sauté for 5 minutes, stirring occasionally.

3. After 5 minutes add the beans, pasta, and bone broth, in that order.

4. Lock lid, set vent to sealing, then set on Manual at high pressure for 6 minutes.

5. Release the pressure manually when cooking time is over.

Favorite memory of sharing this recipe:

My daddy loved making this for us. Every time he made it, he added something different to his basic recipe, which is exactly what can be done to this. Add some frozen peas, add corn, add green beans, whatever you want. It's definitely a great comfort food that warms your heart from the inside.

Serving suggestion:

Serve with a buttered roll and topped with fresh grated Parmesan cheese, or heck, even cheese crisps for a nice crunch.

Kid-Friendly Mac & Cheese with Kale

Makes 6–8 servings

Cynthia Hockman-Chupp, Canby, OR

Prep. Time: 5 minutes ⚜ *Cooking Time: 20 minutes* ⚜ *Setting: Manual*
Pressure: High ⚜ *Release: Manual*

1 lb. dried elbow macaroni

2 Tbsp. butter

½ tsp. curry powder

½ tsp. dry mustard powder

1 tsp. hot pepper sauce

2 tsp. salt

4 cups water

12-oz. can evaporated milk

16 oz. shredded cheddar cheese

6 oz. shredded Parmesan cheese

Optional additions:

1 Tbsp. yellow mustard

1–2 cups frozen/thawed, chopped kale
or spinach

1. Place first 7 ingredients in the inner pot of the Instant Pot: macaroni, butter, curry power, dry mustard powder, hot pepper sauce, salt, water.

2. Cook on Manual at high pressure for 4 minutes. Quick release the pressure when cooking time ends.

3. Leave pot in Keep Warm mode while you stir in evaporated milk. Then, stir in the cheeses gradually, melting each handful as you go.

4. Optional additions: Add 1 Tbsp. yellow mustard and kale or spinach to finished macaroni and cheese. I usually thaw 1–2 cups of frozen, chopped kale and add it to the final product.

Favorite memory of sharing this recipe:

This mac & cheese recipe is faster than fast food! After a day of working away from home, I can throw this in the Instant Pot and have dinner made in minutes. No watching the pot boil!

Instant Pot
TIPS

• The Instant Pot is probably the most versatile cooking appliance I own. I go from making yogurt to rice to mac & cheese to main dishes.

• It's kid-friendly. Using the Instant Pot, kids can easily make recipes that they might not otherwise be able to do with regular appliances.

Honey Lemon Garlic Salmon

Makes 4 servings

Judy Gascho, Woodburn, OR

Prep. Time: 15 minutes ☙ Cooking Time: 8 minutes ☙ Setting: Manual
Pressure: High ☙ Release: Manual

5 Tbsp. olive oil

3 Tbsp. honey

2–3 Tbsp. lemon juice

3 cloves garlic, minced

4 3–4-oz. fresh salmon filets

salt and pepper to taste

1–2 Tbsp. minced parsley (dried or fresh)

lemon slices, *optional*

NOTE
from the cook
If you have a large filet, you can cut it into serving pieces with your kitchen shears.

1. Mix olive oil, honey, lemon juice, and minced garlic in a bowl.

2. Place each piece of salmon on a piece of foil big enough to wrap up the piece of fish.

3. Brush each filet generously with the olive oil mixture.

4. Sprinkle with salt, pepper, and parsley flakes.

5. Top each with a thin slice of lemon, if desired.

6. Wrap each filet and seal well at top.

7. Place 1½ cups of water in the inner pot of your Instant Pot and place the trivet in the pot.

8. Place wrapped filets on the trivet.

9. Close the lid and turn valve to sealing.

10. Cook on Manual at high pressure for 5–8 minutes for smaller pieces, or 10–12 minutes if they are large.

11. Carefully release pressure manually at the end of the cooking time.

12. Unwrap and enjoy.

Side Dishes & Vegetables

Simple Salted Carrots

Makes 4 servings

Hope Comerford, Clinton Township, MI

Prep. Time: 5 minutes ⚜ *Cooking Time: 2 minutes* ⚜ *Setting: Manual then Sauté*
Pressure: High ⚜ *Release: Manual*

1-lb. package baby carrots
1 cup water
1 Tbsp. unsalted butter
sea salt to taste

1. Combine the carrots and water in the inner pot of the Instant Pot.

2. Seal the lid and make sure the vent is on sealing. Select Manual for 2 minutes.

3. When cooking time is done, release the pressure manually, then pour the carrots into a strainer.

4. Wipe the inner pot dry. Select the Sauté function and add the butter.

5. When the butter is melted, add the carrots back into the inner pot and sauté them until they are coated well with the butter.

6. Remove the carrots and sprinkle them with the sea salt to taste before serving.

Brown Sugar Glazed Carrots

Makes 10 servings

Michele Ruvola, Vestal, NY

Prep. Time: 5 minutes ❧ *Cooking Time: 4 minutes* ❧ *Setting: Steam*
Pressure: High ❧ *Release: Manual*

32-oz. bag of baby carrots
½ cup vegetable broth
½ cup brown sugar
4 Tbsp. butter
½ Tbsp. salt

1. Place all ingredients in inner pot of the Instant Pot.

2. Secure the lid, turn valve to sealing, and set timer for 4 minutes on Manual at high pressure.

3. When cooking time is up, perform a quick release to release pressure.

4. Stir carrots, then serve.

Baked Navy Beans

Makes 8 servings

Colleen Heatwole, Burton, MI

Prep. Time: 15 minutes ♣ Cooking Time: 25 minutes ♣ Setting: Manual then Slow Cook
Pressure: High ♣ Release: Natural then Manual

1 lb. navy beans, cleaned, rinsed, soaked overnight in 8 cups water mixed with 1 Tbsp. salt

10 oz. (about 8 slices) thick sliced bacon, cut into ½-inch pieces

1 large onion, chopped

2½ cups water

½ cup molasses

¼ cup brown sugar

1 tsp. dry mustard

½ tsp. salt

¼ tsp. ground black pepper

½ cup ketchup

1. Using Sauté function, cook bacon in the inner pot of the Instant Pot until crisp, about 5 minutes, stirring frequently.

2. Remove bacon using slotted spoon and place on plate lined with paper towels.

3. Cook the onion in bacon fat left in the inner pot until tender, about 3 minutes, stirring frequently and scraping up the brown bits on the bottom of the pot as the onion cooks.

4. Add water, molasses, ketchup, brown sugar, dry mustard, salt, and pepper and stir to combine. Stir in the soaked beans.

5. Secure lid and make sure vent is on sealing. Select Manual at high pressure and set for 25 minutes cook time.

6. When timer on pot beeps, let pressure release natrually for 10 minutes, then do a quick release for the remaining pressure.

7. Discard any beans floating on top. Check beans for tenderness. If not done, pressure cook a few minutes longer.

8. Stir in cooked bacon. Using Slow Cooker function, cook beans uncovered until sauce is desired consistency. Stir frequently to avoid burning the sauce.

NOTE
from the cook

Beans vary in length of time needed to cook, depending on age and variety. Soaked beans cook faster and have slightly more desirable consistency after cooking.

Favorite memory of sharing this recipe:
We use more beans in the winter, but baked beans are a favorite year-round.

Baked Pinto Beans

Makes 8 servings

Janie Steele, Moore, OK

Prep. Time: 15 minutes ⚬ *Cooking Time: 1 hour 30 minutes* ⚬ *Setting: Bean/Chili and Sauté*
Pressure: High ⚬ *Release: Natural*

1 lb. dry pinto beans
1 Tbsp. salt
6 cups water
6 slices bacon, diced
1 onion, diced
¾ cup molasses
½ cup brown sugar
1½ tsp. dry mustard
¾ cup ketchup
½ tsp. salt
½ tsp. garlic
1½ tsp. white wine vinegar
½ tsp. chili powder
½ tsp. Worcestershire sauce

1. Put beans, salt, and water in the inner pot of the Instant Pot.

2. Secure the lid and make sure vent is at sealing. Press the Bean/Chili setting and set on normal for 1 hour.

3. Let the pressure release naturally, then drain the beans. Remove the beans from the pot and set aside.

4. Sauté the bacon and onion in inner pot until the bacon is crisp and onion is translucent.

5. Mix seasonings in a bowl

6. Return beans to pot; stir.

7. Pour seasonings over beans, then stir.

8. Secure the lid and make sure vent is at sealing. Press the Bean/Chili setting and set for 30 minutes.

9. Let pressure release naturally then remove lid. Let sit to thicken.

Best Baked Beans

Makes 8 servings

Carol Eveleth, Cheyenne, WY

Prep. Time: 10 minutes ⚬ Cooking Time: 80 minutes ⚬ Setting: Manual then Sauté
Pressure: High ⚬ Release: Natural

1 lb. dried pinto beans soaked overnight for 8–16 hours

12 cups cold water, divided

2 Tbsp. butter

1 small onion, diced

2 cloves garlic, finely chopped

1½ tsp. salt

12 oz. ketchup

½ cup water

1 Tbsp. Worcestershire sauce

1 cup brown sugar

½ tsp. liquid smoke

3 Polish sausages, chopped

Serving suggestion:
Serve these delicious sweet and smoky baked beans as a side dish at your barbecue, picnics, potlucks, or dinner.

1. Overnight Soaking Method: Place 1 pound dried pinto beans in a large container. Pour 6 cups cold water in the large container and give it a few stirs. Allow beans to soak overnight for 8–16 hours. If your house is very warm, place the large container in the fridge to avoid fermentation.

2. Quick Soaking Method: If you're short on time or forgot to soak the beans overnight, you can use this quick soaking method instead. (The result will not be as good as the overnight soaking method.) Place 1 pound dried pinto beans and 6 cups cold water in the inner pot of the Instant Pot. Close lid, make sure vent is at sealing, and pressure cook on Manual at high pressure for 15 minutes. Let the pressure release naturally.

3. Drain beans: Discard the soaked water and drain the pinto beans through a mesh strainer.

4. Place soaked beans back in the pot and cover with water. Close lid, make sure vent is at sealing, and pressure cook on Manual at high pressure for 20 minutes. Let the pressure release naturally for 2 minutes. After 2 minutes, turn the venting knob to venting position to release the remaining pressure manually. Open the lid carefully.

5. Drain beans. Keep beans in separate bowl.

6. Press Sauté button. Put butter in the inner pot. Add in diced onion and sauté for a minute. Add in chopped garlic cloves and sauté until fragrant (about 30 seconds).

7. Add cooked pinto beans back to the inner pot.

8. Add salt, ketchup, water, Worcestershire sauce, brown sugar, liquid smoke, and chopped Polish sausages to the beans. Mix well. Close lid, make sure vent is at sealing, and cook on Manual at high pressure for 20 minutes. Let the pressure release naturally for 20 minutes. After 20 minutes, turn the venting knob to venting position to release the remaining pressure manually. Open the lid carefully.

Old Fashioned Ham 'n' Beans

Makes 8 servings

Carolyn Spohn, Shawnee, KS

Prep. Time: 20 minutes ❧ Cooking Time: 30–35 minutes ❧ Setting: Meat or Soup/Stew
Pressure: High ❧ Release: Natural or Manual

meaty ham bone (with as much fat removed as possible) or 2–3 ham hocks

2 cups great northern beans, sorted and rinsed

2 medium carrots, chopped

1 medium onion, chopped

2 stalks celery, chopped

2 cloves garlic, sliced or minced

4–6 cups broth or water (depending on how "brothy" you want your beans)

finely chopped onion for garnish, *optional*

1. Place all ingredients in the inner pot of the Instant Pot, except for finely chopped onion. Seal the lid, make sure vent is at sealing, and cook on either the Meat or Stew/Soup setting for 30 to 35 minutes.

2. Release pressure manually or let it release naturally.

3. Check beans to be sure fully cooked. If necessary, pressure cook a while longer, and release pressure same as in step 2.

4. Remove ham bone or hocks and trim off the skin, bone, gristle and visible fat. Return meat to cooker and leave on Keep Warm setting.

5. Serve with chopped onion as a garnish if desired.

Serving suggestion:
Very good with cornbread.

Favorite memory of sharing this recipe:
I grew up at the end of the Great Depression and this was a favorite meal at that time. Ham was relatively cheap and a big pot of ham 'n' beans could last for another meal.

Mashed Potatoes

Makes 3–4 servings

Colleen Heatwole, Burton, MI

Prep. Time: 10 minutes ❧ Cooking Time: 5 minutes ❧ Setting: Manual
Pressure: High ❧ Release: Manual

1 cup water

6 medium size potatoes, peeled and quartered

2 Tbsp. unsalted butter

½ to ¾ cup milk, warmed

salt and pepper to taste

1. Add 1 cup water to the inner pot of the Instant Pot. Put the steamer basket in the pot and place potatoes in the basket.

2. Seal the lid and make sure vent is at sealing. Using Manual mode, select 5 minutes cook time, high pressure.

3. When cook time ends, do a manual release. Use a fork to test potatoes. If needed, relock lid and cook at high pressure a few minutes more.

4. Transfer potatoes to large mixing bowl. Mash using hand mixer, stirring in butter. Gradually add warmed milk. Season with salt and pepper to taste.

Favorite memory of sharing this recipe:

I learned how to mash potatoes a long time ago using tips from an aunt's cookbook. Milk must always be warmed and added gradually, not all at once.

NOTE

from the cook

A few lumps are okay . . . that lets you know they are real potatoes. Some people prefer a ricer to a hand mixer for perfect, lump-free mashed potatoes. I used to do it that way, but my family is fine with hand-mixer mashed potatoes.

Potatoes with Parsley

Makes 4 servings

Colleen Heatwole, Burton, MI

Prep. Time: 10 minutes ⚬ *Cooking Time: 5 minutes* ⚬ *Setting: Sauté then Manual*
Pressure: High ⚬ *Release: Manual*

3 Tbsp. butter, *divided*

2 lbs. medium red potatoes (about 2 oz. each), halved lengthwise

1 clove garlic, minced

½ tsp. salt

½ cup chicken broth

2 Tbsp. chopped fresh parsley

1. Place 1 Tbsp. butter in the inner pot of the Instant Pot and select Sauté.

2. After butter is melted, add potatoes, garlic, and salt, stirring well.

3. Sauté 4 minutes, stirring frequently.

4. Add chicken broth and stir well.

5. Seal lid, make sure vent is on sealing, then select Manual for 5 minutes on high pressure.

6. When cooking time is up, manually release the pressure.

7. Strain potatoes, toss with remaining 2 Tbsp. butter and chopped parsley, and serve immediately.

NOTE
from the cook

We raise potatoes in our garden—Yukon gold, Kennebec, and red ones. This works well for all types of potatoes and is best with new potatoes.

Bacon Ranch Red Potatoes

Makes 6 servings

Hope Comerford, Clinton Township, MI

Prep. Time: 15 minutes ⚓ Cooking Time: 7 minutes ⚓ Setting: Sauté then Manual
Pressure: High ⚓ Release: Manual

4 strips bacon, chopped into small pieces

2 lbs. red potatoes, diced

1 Tbsp. fresh chopped parsley

1 tsp. sea salt

4 cloves garlic, chopped

1-oz. packet ranch dressing/seasoning mix

⅓ cup water

½ cup shredded sharp white cheddar

2 Tbsp. chopped green onions for garnish

1. Set the Instant Pot to Sauté, add the bacon to the inner pot, and cook until crisp.

2. Stir in the potatoes, parsley, sea salt, garlic, ranch dressing seasoning, and water.

3. Secure the lid, make sure vent is at sealing, then set the Instant Pot to Manual for 7 minutes at high pressure.

4. When cooking time is up, do a quick release and carefully open the lid.

5. Stir in the cheese. Garnish with the green onions.

Sweet Potato Puree

Makes 4–6 servings

Colleen Heatwole, Burton, MI

Prep. Time: 10 minutes ☘ *Cooking Time: 6 minutes* ☘ *Setting: Manual*
Pressure: High ☘ *Release: Manual*

3 lbs. sweet potatoes, peeled and cut into roughly 2-inch cubes

1 cup water

2 Tbsp. butter

1 tsp. salt

2 tsp. packed brown sugar

2 tsp. lemon juice

½ tsp. cinnamon

⅛ tsp. nutmeg, *optional*

1. Place sweet potatoes and water in inner pot of the Instant Pot.

2. Secure the lid, make sure vent is at sealing, then cook for 6 minutes on high using the Manual setting.

3. Manually release the pressure when cook time is up.

4. Drain sweet potatoes and place in large mixing bowl. Mash with potato masher or hand mixer.

5. Once thoroughly mashed, add remaining ingredients.

6. Taste and adjust seasonings to taste.

7. Serve immediately while still hot.

NOTE
from the cook

We raise sweet potatoes and this is a good way to cook them.

Perfect Sweet Potatoes

Makes 4–6 servings

Brittney Horst, Lititz, PA

Prep. Time: 5 minutes ❧ *Cooking Time: 15 minutes* ❧ *Setting: Manual*
Pressure: High ❧ *Release: Natural*

4–6 medium sweet potatoes

1 cup of water

1. Scrub skin of sweet potatoes with a brush until clean. Pour water into inner pot of the Instant Pot. Place steamer basket in the bottom of the inner pot. Place sweet potatoes on top of steamer basket.

2. Secure the lid and turn valve to seal.

3. Select the manual mode and set to Pressure Cook on high for 15 minutes.

4. Allow pressure to release naturally (about 10 minutes).

5. Once the pressure valve lowers, remove lid and serve immediately.

Instant Pot
TIPS

• Not necessarily pertinent to this recipe, but on the newest version of the Instant Pot that I have, the Sauté feature seems to get SUPER hot. Not sure I recommend sautéing anything without a lot of oil/liquid—or just avoid it all together. Several recipes call for it but then my Instant Pot said "burn" on it and stopped cooking because the onions and garlic were burning at the bottom. I feel like it gets hot enough without having to sauté anything like onions and garlic beforehand. Maybe the original versions are less hot, but people should be aware of what version they have.

• Super large sweet potatoes need more than 15 minutes! I tried one mega sweet potato and it was not cooked in the center. Maybe 20 minutes will do.

These also make an easy side dish and your family can dress them up individually, or you can then create an easy baked sweet potato casserole without waiting for water to boil on the stove.

NOTE
from the cook

You can store cooked sweet potatoes in the fridge for 3–4 days in an airtight container.

Favorite memory of sharing this recipe:
My eleven-month-old daughter LOVES sweet potatoes and I make these all the time for her. She will spit out sweet potatoes from the microwave but will devour them from the Instant Pot or oven!

Perfect White Rice

Makes 4 servings

Hope Comerford, Clinton Township, MI

Prep. Time: 2 minutes ❦ Cooking Time: 8 minutes ❦ Setting: Rice
Pressure: High ❦ Release: Natural then Manual

1 cup uncooked white rice

1 tsp. grapeseed, olive oil, or coconut oil

1 cup water

pinch of salt

1. Rinse rice under cold running water until the water runs clear, then pour into the inner pot.

2. Add oil, water, and salt to the inner pot.

3. Lock the lid and set the steam valve to its sealing position. Select the Rice button and set to cook for 8 minutes.

4. Allow the pressure to release naturally for 10 minutes and then release any remaining pressure manually.

5. Fluff the rice with a fork and serve.

Rice Guiso

Makes 3–6 servings

Cynthia Hockman-Chupp, Canby, OR

Prep. Time: 5 minutes ❧ *Cooking Time: 15 minutes* ❧ *Setting: Rice*
Pressure: High ❧ *Release: Natural or Manual*

1 Tbsp. oil (I prefer coconut)

1 onion, chopped

1 cup rice

1 tsp. salt

⅛ tsp. pepper

¼–½ cup chopped bell pepper, any color (or a variety of colors!)

1–1⅛ cups water

2 Tbsp. tomato paste

1. Place all ingredients in inner pot of the Instant Pot. Stir.

2. Secure the lid and make sure vent is at sealing. Push rice button and set for 15 minutes. Allow to cook.

3. Use manual release for a final product that is more moist, natural release for a slightly drier rice. I prefer natural release for this rice.

Favorite memory of sharing this recipe:

This is a modification of a long-time favorite from More-with-Less. I've used that recipe in our family for more than twenty years, usually with chicken enchiladas, an all-around favorite meal. I tried it in the Instant Pot and learned that I could make it quicker and not have to hover over it. I'm done making it on the stovetop! :)

Instant Pot TIP

For this recipe and other rice recipes, I usually use a 1:1 ratio of rice to water. I sometimes find I need to slightly tweak it with a little more water, perhaps depending on the water content of other ingredients.

NOTE
from the cook

I chop and freeze bell peppers in the summer and put them in small freezer bags. They are ideal for this recipe. I dump them straight into the pot from the freezer. No thawing.

Perfect Basmati Rice

Makes 3–6 servings

Carol Eveleth, Cheyenne, WY

Prep. Time: 1 minute 🔹 Cooking Time: 24 minutes 🔹 Setting: Manual
Pressure: High 🔹 Release: Natural then Manual

1 cup water
1 cup basmati rice

1. Place 1 cup of basmati rice and 1 cup of water into the inner pot of the Instant Pot. (If you're rinsing the rice, it'll throw off the rice-to-water ratio. So, be sure to reduce 3 tablespoons of water from the 1 cup of water stated in the recipe.)

2. Close lid, turn valve to sealing, and cook on Manual at high pressure for 6 minutes. Turn off the heat and do a 10-minute natural release. Release the remaining pressure (if any) and open the lid carefully.

3. Fluff the rice with a rice spatula or fork, then serve with your favorite main dish, or enjoy alone!

NOTE
from the cook
If you enjoy softer rice, increase the liquid amount rather than cooking time.

Best Brown Rice

Makes 6–12 servings

Colleen Heatwole, Burton, MI

Prep. Time: 5 minutes ❧ Cooking Time: 22 minutes ❧ Setting: Manual
Pressure: High ❧ Release: Natural then Manual

2 cups brown rice

2½ cups water

1. Rinse brown rice in a fine mesh strainer.

2. Add rice and water to the inner pot of the Instant Pot.

3. Secure the lid and make sure vent is on sealing.

4. Use Manual setting and select 22 minutes cooking time on high pressure.

5. When cooking time is done, let the pressure release naturally for 10 minutes, then press Cancel and manually release any remaining pressure.

NOTE
from the cook

• Brown rice is my preferred rice since it is more nutritious than white rice.

• I have also cooked brown rice 25 minutes and then done quick release and it worked fine.

• I don't add salt until it is cooked, and how much I add if any depends on how I'm using the rice.

Brown Rice

Makes 4–7 servings

Marla Folkerts, Batavia, IL

Prep. Time: 4–5 minutes ❧ *Cooking Time: 22–25 minutes* ❧ *Setting: Sauté then Manual*
Pressure: High ❧ *Release: Natural*

½ cup finely diced onion

2 Tbsp. butter

1½ cups brown rice

1¾ cups low-sodium chicken broth

1. Use the Sauté function on the Instant Pot to sauté the diced onion and butter in the inner pot.

2. When the onions are translucent, place everything else in the inner pot.

3. Secure the lid, make sure the vent is at sealing, then use the Manual setting for 22–25 minutes on high pressure.

4. Let the pressure release naturally, then fluff!

Israeli Couscous

Makes 4–8 servings

Colleen Heatwole, Burton, MI

Prep. Time: 5 minutes ⚬ *Cooking Time: 5 minutes* ⚬ *Setting: Sauté then Manual*
Pressure: High ⚬ *Release: Manual*

2 Tbsp. butter

2½ cups chicken broth

16-oz. pkg. Trader Joe's Harvest Grains Blend couscous (available at Trader Joe's and Amazon. If other couscous is used, see adjustment of cooking time in directions.)

salt and pepper to taste

1. Melt butter using Sauté function.

2. Add chicken broth and couscous to the Inner Pot. Stir to combine.

3. Lock lid in place, make sure vent is at sealing, then use Manual function and cook on high pressure for 5 minutes. (If substituting a different brand of couscous, cook for one half of the recommended time listed on the package.)

4. When time is up, do a quick release.

5. Fluff with a fork and add salt and pepper to taste.

NOTE
from the cook

While I hesitate to recommend brand name items, I was exceedingly happy to be told about this recipe for Harvest Grains Blend. We don't live near Trader Joe's, but I buy it there whenever I can. Trader Joe's Harvest Grains Blend is truly a "savory blend of Israeli style couscous, orzo, baby garbanzo beans and red quinoa."

Instant Pot
TIP

I find that I use the Manual setting on my Instant Pot for almost everything, and just adjust that for the cooking time.

Quinoa with Almonds and Cranberries

Makes 4 servings

Colleen Heatwole, Burton, MI

Prep. Time: 5 minutes ☙ Cooking Time: 2 minutes ☙ Setting: Manual
Pressure: High ☙ Release: Natural then Manual

1 cup quinoa, rinsed well

½ cup roasted slivered almonds

1 bouillon cube, chicken or beef

1½ cups water

¼ tsp. salt, *optional*

1 cinnamon stick

½ cup dried cranberries or cherries

1 bay leaf

1. Add all ingredients to the inner pot of the Instant Pot.

2. Secure the lid and make sure vent is on sealing. Cook 2 minutes using high pressure in Manual mode.

3. Turn off pot and let the pressure release naturally for 10 minutes. After 10 minutes are up, release pressure manually.

4. Remove cinnamon stick and bay leaf.

5. Fluff with fork and serve.

Favorite memory of sharing this recipe:

My daughter is a real fan of this dish. It closely resembles the recipe on the quinoa package I have, but is now adapted for Instant Pot.

NOTE
from the cook
I omit the salt because bouillon cubes are salty.

Orange-Honey Cranberry Sauce

Makes 6–8 servings

Brittney Horst, Lititz, PA

Prep. Time: 5 minutes ❧ *Cooking Time: 10 minutes* ❧ *Setting: Manual and Sauté*
Pressure: High ❧ *Release: Natural*

3 cups fresh cranberries

½ cup orange juice (about 2 medium oranges)

½ cup 100% apple cider

1 Tbsp. orange zest

pinch pumpkin pie spice

¼ tsp. salt

Sauté ingredients:

¼ cup amaretto, *optional*

⅔ cup honey

1. Add the cranberries, orange juice, apple cider, orange zest, pumpkin pie spice, and salt to the inner pot of your Instant Pot. Put on the lid and set the vent to sealed. Cook on high pressure on Manual mode for 6 minutes.

2. Let the pressure release naturally.

3. Once pressure has completely released, remove lid, press the Cancel button to turn off the Instant Pot, then press the Sauté button and the adjust button until it sets to "less."

4. Add in the sauté ingredients. Mix well with a large spoon and mash the fruit pieces as you go.

5. Cook until it reaches the thickness you desire, then turn off and store in fridge once cooled.

Serving suggestion:

Great for an easy make-ahead side dish for a holiday meal!

Desserts & Beverages

*SPECIAL NOTE FROM HOPE: You will want a sealing ring to use JUST for "sweets."
The sealing rings tend to hold odors, which will leach into your foods. (You don't want your
sweets to taste like pork, or whatever else you cooked before it!)

Chocolate Pots de Crème

Makes 6–7 servings

Judy Gascho, Woodburn, OR

Prep. Time: 20 minutes ✂ Cooking Time: 6 minutes ✂ Setting: Manual
Pressure: High ✂ Release: Natural then Manual

1½ cups heavy cream

½ cup whole milk

8 oz. unsweetened baking chocolate

5 large egg yolks

¼ cup sugar

pinch salt

whipped cream and grated chocolate for garnish, *optional*

1. In a small saucepan, bring the cream and milk to a simmer.

2. Melt chocolate at 50% power in 30-second increments in microwave, stirring after each increment.

3. In a large mixing bowl, whisk together egg yolks, sugar, and salt. Slowly whisk in hot cream and milk. Whisk in melted chocolate until blended.

4. Pour into 6–7 custard cups. Wrap each tightly with foil.

5. Add 1½ cups water to the inner pot of the Instant Pot and place the trivet in the bottom.

6. Place 3–4 wrapped cups on the trivet. Place a second trivet on top of the cups and place the remaining cups on the second trivet. (If you don't have a second trivet, place the remaining cups staggered on the top of the bottom layer of cups.)

7. Lock the lid in place and make sure vent is at sealing. Select high pressure in Manual mode and set the timer for 6 minutes. When cooking time is up, turn off the pressure cooker and let the pressure release for 15 minutes naturally, then do a quick pressure release to release any remaining pressure. When the valve drops, carefully remove lid.

8. Carefully remove the cups to a wire rack and remove foil immediately. Cool.

9. When cool, refrigerate cups covered with plastic wrap for at least 4 hours or overnight.

NOTE
from the cook

It is important to tightly wrap with foil when cooking or they will have water on top of them.

Dump Cake

Makes 8–10 servings

Janie Steele, Moore, OK

Prep. Time: 10 minutes ☙ Cooking Time: 12 minutes ☙ Setting: Manual
Pressure: High ☙ Release: Manual

6 Tbsp. butter
1 box cake mix (I used spice)
2 20-oz. cans pie filling (I used apple)

1. Mix butter and dry cake mix in bowl. It will be clumpy.

2. Pour pie filling in the inner pot of the Instant Pot.

3. Pour the dry mix over top.

4. Secure lid and make sure vent is at sealing. Cook for 12 minutes on Manual mode at high pressure.

5. Release pressure manually when cook time is up and remove lid to prevent condensation from getting into cake.

6. Let stand 5–10 minutes.

Serving suggestion:
Serve with ice cream.

Cookies & Cream Cheesecake (Gluten-Free)

Makes 6 servings

Hope Comerford, Clinton Township, MI

Prep. Time: 15 minutes ⚜ Cooking Time: 35 minutes ⚜ Setting: Manual
Pressure: High ⚜ Release: Natural then Manual

Crust:

12 whole gluten-free chocolate sandwich cookies, crushed into crumbs

2 Tbsp. salted butter, melted

Cheesecake:

16 oz. cream cheese, room temperature

½ cup granulated sugar

2 large eggs, room temperature

1 Tbsp. gluten-free all-purpose flour

¼ cup heavy cream

2 tsp. pure vanilla extract

8 whole gluten-free chocolate sandwich cookies, coarsely chopped

Toppings:

1 cup whipping cream, whipped

8 whole gluten-free chocolate sandwich cookies, coarsely chopped

chocolate sauce, *optional*

1. Tightly wrap in foil the bottom of 7-inch springform pan. Spray the inside with nonstick cooking spray.

2. In a small bowl, stir together the 12 crushed gluten-free chocolate sandwich cookies and melted butter. Press the crumbs into the bottom of the prepared pan. (I find the bottom of a glass cup is a great tool to use for this.) Place this in the freezer for 10–15 minutes.

3. In a large bowl, beat the cream cheese until smooth. (You can use an electric mixer, or stand mixer with paddle attachment.)

4. Add the sugar and mix until combined.

5. Add the eggs, one at a time, making sure each is fully incorporated before adding the next. Be sure to scrape down the bowl in between each egg.

6. Add in the flour, heavy cream, and vanilla and continue to mix until smooth.

7. Gently fold in the 8 chopped gluten-free chocolate sandwich cookies and pour this batter into the pan you had in the freezer.

8. Cover the top of the pan with a piece of foil.

9. Pour 1½ cups of water into the inner pot and place the trivet in the bottom of the pot.

10. Create a "foil sling" by folding a 20-inch long piece of foil in half lengthwise two times. This

"sling" will allow you to easily place and remove the springform pan from the pot.

11. Place the cheesecake pan in the center of the sling and carefully lower the pan into the inner pot. Fold down the excess foil from the sling to ensure the pot closes properly.

12. Lock the lid into place and make sure the vent is at sealing. Press the Manual button and cook on high pressure for 35 minutes.

13. When the Instant Pot beeps, hit the Keep Warm/Cancel button to turn off the pressure cooker. Allow the pressure to release naturally for 10 minutes and then do a quick release to release any pressure remaining in the pot.

14. Carefully remove the lid. Gently unfold the foil sling and remove the cheesecake from the pot to a cooling rack using the foil sling "handles." Uncover the cheesecake and allow it to cool to room temperature.

15. Once the cheesecake has cooled, refrigerate it for at least 8 hours, or overnight.

16. Before serving, top with whipped cream, chopped gluten-free chocolate sandwich cookies, and a drizzle of chocolate sauce if desired.

Rice Pudding

Makes 6–8 servings

Michele Ruvola, Vestal, NY

Prep. Time: 3 minutes ⚹ *Cooking Time: 20 minutes* ⚹ *Setting: Manual then Sauté*
Pressure: High ⚹ *Release: Natural then Manual*

1 cup arborio rice
1½ cups water
¼ tsp. salt
2 cups whole milk, *divided*
½ cup sugar
2 eggs
½ tsp. vanilla extract
Optional toppings: cinnamon, or toasted coconut and pineapple tidbits for a twist of piña colada rice pudding

1. Place rice, water, and salt into the inner pot of the Instant Pot.

2. Lock lid, make sure vent is at sealing, and select Manual at high pressure and 3 minutes cook time.

3. Let the pressure release naturally for 10 minutes, then manually release the remaining pressure.

4. Add 1½ cups of milk and sugar to rice in pot. Stir to combine.

5. In a bowl, whisk eggs with remaining ½ cup of milk and vanilla extract.

6. Pour through fine mesh strainer into the inner pot of rice to take out any lumps.

7. Select Sauté and cook, stirring constantly so milk does not burn or rice stick. Stir until mixture boils. Turn off pot.

8. Serve warm or cold.

9. Top with optional toppings, if desired.

Favorite memory of sharing this recipe: Back in the day when I was a little girl, every time I made rice pudding, I always remember having to stir the pot to make sure the milk did not burn or boil over. I would constantly ask my mom, "Is it ready yet?" It was never fast enough for me!

NOTE
from the cook
Pudding will thicken as it cools.

Buttery Rice Pudding

Makes 6–8 servings

Janie Steele, Moore, OK

Prep. Time: 5 minutes ⚭ *Cooking Time: 14 minutes* ⚭ *Setting: Sauté and Manual*
Pressure: High ⚭ *Release: Natural*

1 ½ Tbsp. butter
1 cup uncooked rice
½ cup sugar
1 cup water
2 cups milk (2% works best)
1 egg
¼ cup evaporated milk
½ tsp. vanilla extract
½ tsp. almond extract, *optional*
nutmeg, *optional*
cinnamon, *optional*

1. In the inner pot of the Instant Pot, melt butter using the Sauté setting. Add the rice, sugar, water, and milk, then stir.

2. Secure lid and make sure vent is at sealing. Cook on Manual on high pressure for 14 minutes. Let the pressure release naturally when cook time is up.

3. In a bowl whisk together the egg and evaporated milk.

4. Take a spoon of rice mixture and add slowly to egg mixture.

5. Return all to the inner pot and stir in the vanilla and optional almond extract.

6. Use the Sauté function and bring mixture to bubble for 30–60 seconds.

7. Stir slowly so it does not stick to the pot.

8. Use nutmeg or cinnamon to garnish if desired.

Creamy Rice Pudding

Makes 10 servings

Colleen Heatwole, Burton, MI

Prep. Time: 5 minutes ⚜ *Cooking Time: 15 minutes* ⚜ *Setting: Sauté then Manual*
Pressure: Low ⚜ *Release: Manual*

1½ cups arborio rice

2 cups milk (2% or whole)

14-oz. can coconut milk, light preferred

1 cup water

½ cup granulated sugar

2 tsp. cinnamon

½ tsp. salt

1½ tsp. vanilla extract

1 cup dried tart cherries or golden raisins

1. Rinse rice and drain.

2. Place rice, milk, coconut milk, water, sugar, cinnamon, and salt in the inner pot of the Instant Pot.

3. Select Sauté and bring to boil, stirring constantly to dissolve sugar.

4. As soon as mixture comes to a boil, turn off Sauté.

5. Secure lid and make sure vent is at sealing. Using Manual mode, select 15 minutes and low pressure.

6. When cook time is up, manually release the pressure.

7. Remove lid and add vanilla and dried fruit. Stir.

8. Place cover on pot but do not turn on.

9. Let stand for 15 minutes, then stir and serve.

Baked Apples

Makes 6 servings

Judy Gascho, Woodburn, OR

Prep. Time: 15 minutes ⁂ *Cooking Time: 9 minutes* ⁂ *Setting: Manual*
Pressure: High ⁂ *Release: Natural then Manual*

6 medium apples, cored
1 cup apple juice or cider
¼ cup raisins or dried cranberries
½ cup brown sugar
1 tsp. cinnamon

1. Put the apples into the inner pot of the Instant Pot.

2. Pour in the apple juice or cider. Sprinkle the raisins, brown sugar, and cinnamon over the apples.

3. Close and lock the lid and be sure the steam vent is in the sealing position.

4. Cook for 9 minutes on Manual mode at high pressure.

5. When time is up, unplug and turn off the pressure cooker. Let pressure release naturally for 15 minutes, then manually release any remaining pressure.

6. Take off lid and remove apples to individual small bowls, adding cooking liquid to each.

Apple Sauce

Makes 16 servings

Colleen Heatwole, Burton, MI

Prep. Time: 20 minutes ⚶ *Cooking Time: 5 minutes* ⚶ *Setting: Manual*
Pressure: High ⚶ *Release: Natural then Manual*

10 large soft apples (such as Jonagold, Golden Delicious, Rome, or Fuji), peeled and sliced

¼ cup apple juice or water

1 tsp. ground cinnamon

¼ cup sugar, *optional*

1. Combine all ingredients except sugar in the inner pot of the Instant Pot and stir to combine.

2. Secure the lid and make sure vent is on sealing. Press Manual mode; set to 4 minutes at high pressure.

3. After cook time is up, let the pressure release naturally for 5 minutes, then release the rest of the pressure manually.

4. Stir apples, breaking up large chunks, or blend with immersion blender.

5. Taste for sweetness and add sugar if desired.

Favorite memory of sharing this recipe:

We love applesauce, especially slightly chunky, and this is a wonderful way to prepare it.

The grandchildren especially like this applesauce and it has "filled out" many meals.

NOTE
from the cook

Many apples are sweet enough without extra sugar.

Cider

Makes 6–8 servings

Anita Troyer, Fairview, MI

Prep. Time: 10 minutes ❧ Cooking Time: 4 hours ❧ Setting: Slow Cook

7 medium Gala or Honeycrisp apples

2 pears

1 orange

3 cinnamon sticks

1 tsp. whole cloves

½ tsp. whole allspice

1 star anise

12 cups water

½ cup brown sugar

1. Wash all the fruit and quarter without coring or peeling, including the orange.

2. Place the fruit and the rest of the ingredients into the Instant Pot inner pot.

3. Secure the lid. Select Slow Cook setting and set for 3 hours.

4. When cook time is up, use a masher to break up the fruit and stir well. Set timer for 1 more hour on Slow Cook setting.

5. Strain through a fine sieve and put into a pitcher. Add sugar according to your taste.

Serving suggestion:
Serve warm.

Metric Equivalent Measurements

dash = little less than ⅛ tsp.

3 tsp. = 1 Tbsp.

2 Tbsp. = 1 oz.

4 Tbsp. = ¼ cup

5 Tbsp. plus 1 tsp. = ⅓ cup

8 Tbsp. = ½ cup

12 Tbsp. = ¾ cup

16 Tbsp. = 1 cup

1 cup = 8 oz. liquid

2 cups = 1 pt.

4 cups = 1 qt.

4 qt. = 1 gal.

1 stick butter = ¼ lb.

1 stick butter = ½ cup

1 stick butter = 8 Tbsp.

beans, 1 lb. dried = 2–2½ cups (depending on the size of the beans)

bell pepper, 1 large = 1 cup chopped

cheese, hard (for example, cheddar, Swiss, Monterey Jack, mozzarella), 1 lb. grated = 4 cups

cheese, cottage, 1 lb. = 2 cups

chocolate chips, 6-oz. pkg. = 1 scant cup

crackers (butter, saltines, snack), 20 single crackers = 1 cup crumbs

herbs, 1 Tbsp. fresh = 1 tsp. dried

lemon, 1 medium-sized = 2–3 Tbsp. juice

lemon, 1 medium-sized = 2–3 tsp. grated rind

mustard, 1 Tbsp. prepared = 1 tsp. dry or ground mustard

oatmeal, 1 lb. dry = about 5 cups dry

onion, 1 medium-sized = ½ cup chopped

Pasta

macaroni, penne, and other small or tubular shapes, 1 lb. dry = 4 cups uncooked

noodles, 1 lb. dry = 6 cups uncooked

spaghetti, linguine, fettucine, 1 lb. dry = 4 cups uncooked

potatoes, white, 1 lb. = 3 medium-sized potatoes = 2 cups mashed

Potatoes, sweet, 1 lb. = 3 medium-sized potatoes = 2 cups mashed

rice, 1 lb. dry = 2 cups uncooked

sugar, confectioners', 1 lb. = 3½ cups sifted

whipping cream, 1 cup unwhipped = 2 cups whipped

whipped topping, 8-oz. container = 3 cups

yeast, dry, 1 envelope (¼ oz.) = 1 Tbsp.

Assumptions about Ingredients

flour = unbleached or white, and all-purpose

oatmeal or oats = dry, quick or rolled (old-fashioned), unless specified

pepper = black, finely ground

rice = regular, long-grain (not instant unless specified)

salt = table salt

shortening = solid, not liquid

sugar = granulated sugar (not brown and not confectioners')

Substitute Ingredients

For 1 cup buttermilk—use 1 cup plain yogurt; or pour $1^1/_3$ Tbsp. lemon juice or vinegar into a 1-cup measure. Fill the cup with milk. Stir and let stand for 5 minutes. Stir again before using.

For 1 oz. unsweetened baking chocolate—stir together 3 Tbsp. unsweetened cocoa powder and 1 Tbsp. butter, softened.

For 1 Tbsp. cornstarch—use 2 Tbsp. all-purpose flour; or 4 tsp. instant tapioca.

For 1 garlic clove—use ¼ tsp. garlic salt (reduce salt in recipe by $^1/_8$ tsp.); or $^1/_8$ tsp. garlic powder.

For 1 Tbsp. fresh herbs—use 1 tsp. dried herbs.

For 8 oz. fresh mushrooms—use 1 4-oz. can mushrooms, drained.

For 1 Tbsp. prepared mustard—use 1 tsp. dry or ground mustard.

For 1 medium-sized fresh onion—use 2 Tbsp. minced dried onion; or 2 tsp. onion salt (reduce salt in recipe by 1 tsp.); or 1 tsp. onion powder. Note: These substitutions will work for meatballs and meatloaf, but not for sautéing.

For 1 cup sour milk—use 1 cup plain yogurt; or pour 1 Tbsp. lemon juice or vinegar into a 1-cup measure. Fill with milk. Stir and then let stand for 5 minutes. Stir again before using.

For 2 Tbsp. tapioca—use 3 Tbsp. all-purpose flour.

For 1 cup canned tomatoes—use $1^1/_3$ cups diced fresh tomatoes, cooked gently for 10 minutes.

For 1 Tbsp. tomato paste—use 1 Tbsp. ketchup.

For 1 Tbsp. vinegar—use 1 Tbsp. lemon juice.

For 1 cup heavy cream—add $^3/_4$ cup melted butter to ¾ cup milk. Note: This will work for baking and cooking, but not for whipping.

For 1 cup whipping cream—chill thoroughly $^2/_3$ cup evaporated milk, plus the bowl and beaters, then whip; or use 2 cups store-bought whipped topping.

For ½ cup wine—pour 2 Tbsp. wine vinegar into a ½-cup measure. Fill with broth (chicken, beef, or vegetable). Stir and then let stand for 5 minutes. Stir again before using.

Recipe and Ingredient Index

A
almond milk
  Best Steel Cut-Oats, 13
almonds
  Best Steel Cut-Oats, 13
  Quinoa with Almonds and
    Cranberries, 197
Apple Butter, 23
apples
  Baked Apples, 215
  Cider, 219
  Fruit Breakfast Cobbler, 15
  Instant Pot Applesauce, 21
Apple Sauce, 217
artichoke hearts
  Spinach and Artichoke
    Dip, 39
Asian Chicken Noodle Soup, 63

B
bacon
  Baked Navy Beans, 167
  Baked Pinto Beans, 169
  Potato Bacon Soup, 71
  Potato Soup, 75
Bacon Ranch Red Potatoes, 179
Baked Apples, 215
Baked Navy Beans, 167
Baked Pinto Beans, 169
barbecue sauce
  BBQ Pork Sandwiches, 111
  Pork Baby Back Ribs, 117
  Pulled Pork, 109
  Taylor's Favorite Uniquely
    Stuffed Peppers, 151
  Tender Tasty Ribs, 115
BBQ Pork Sandwiches, 111
beans
  black

Black Bean Soup, 81
Ground Turkey Stew, 83
cannellini
  Daddy's Pasta Fasool, 155
chili
  Favorite Chili, 91
great northern
  Old Fashioned Ham 'n'
    Beans, 173
  White Chicken Chili, 89
navy
  Baked Navy Beans, 167
pinto
  Baked Pinto Beans, 169
  Best Baked Beans, 170–171
beef
  Bell Pepper Casserole, 105
  Favorite Chili, 91
  Meatballs, 49
  Philly Cheese Steaks, 103
  Porcupine Meatballs, 51
  Pot Roast, 99
  Quick Steak Tacos, 97
  Unstuffed Cabbage Soup, 65
Beef and Kale Stew, 87
Beef Broccoli, 101
Beef Stew, 84–85
Bell Pepper Casserole, 105
Best Baked Beans, 170–171
Best Steel Cut-Oats, 13
Black Bean Soup, 81
Blackberry Baked Brie, 45
bread
  Cinnamon French Toast
    Casserole, 25
  Philly Cheese Steaks, 103
  Steamed Brown Bread, 29
broccoli
  Beef Broccoli, 101

Chicken Broccoli and Rice, 143
Chicken Cheddar Broccoli
  Soup, 55
Brown Lentil Soup, 77
Brown Rice, 193
Brown Sugar Glazed Carrots, 165
Butter Chicken, 123
Butternut Squash Soup, 79
Buttery Lemon Chicken, 125
Buttery Rice Pudding, 211

C
cabbage
  Asian Chicken Noodle Soup,
    63
  Chicken Vegetable Soup, 59
  Unstuffed Cabbage Soup, 65
cake mix
  Dump Cake, 205
Candied Pecans, 35
Carol's Yogurt, 19
carrots
  Asian Chicken Noodle
    Soup, 63
  Beef Stew, 84–85
  Brown Sugar Glazed Carrots,
    165
  Chicken Cheddar Broccoli
    Soup, 55
  Chicken Noodle Soup, 61
  Chicken Vegetable Soup, 59
  Creamy Chicken Wild Rice
    Soup, 57
  Daddy's Pasta Fasool, 155
  Meatball and Pasta Soup, 67
  Old Fashioned Ham 'n'
    Beans, 173
  Pot Roast, 99
  Simple Salted Carrots, 163

Split Pea Soup, 69
Split Pea Soup with Chicken
    Sausage, 73
cheese
    Brie
        Blackberry Baked Brie, 45
    cheddar
        Bacon Ranch Red
            Potatoes, 179
        Cheesy Stuffed Cabbage,
            149
        Chicken Broccoli and Rice,
            143
        Chicken Cheddar Broccoli
            Soup, 55
        Creamy Jalapeño Dip, 43
        Kid-Friendly Mac &
            Cheese with Kale, 157
        Potato and Corn Chowder,
            93
        Potato Bacon Soup, 71
        Potato Soup, 75
        White Chicken Chili, 89
    Mexican blend
        Quick Steak Tacos, 97
        White Chicken Chili, 89
    Monterey Jack
        Creamy Spinach Dip, 41
    mozzarella
        Cheesy Stuffed Cabbage, 149
        Spinach and Artichoke
            Dip, 39
    Parmesan
        Cheesy Stuffed Cabbage, 149
        Creamy Spinach Dip, 41
        Kid-Friendly Mac &
            Cheese with Kale, 157
        Spinach and Artichoke
            Dip, 39
    provolone
        Philly Cheese Steaks, 103
Cheesy Stuffed Cabbage, 149
cherries, dried
    Best Steel Cut-Oats, 13

Creamy Rice Pudding, 213
chicken
    Asian Chicken Noodle Soup,
        63
    Butter Chicken, 123
    Buttery Lemon Chicken, 125
    Creamy Chicken Wild Rice
        Soup, 57
    Creamy Jalapeño Dip, 43
    Garlic Galore Rotisserie
        Chicken, 121
    Insta Pasta à la Maria, 137
    Lemony Chicken Thighs, 131
    Mild Chicken Curry with
        Coconut Milk, 147
    Orange Chicken Breasts, 133
    Orange Chicken Thighs with
        Bell Peppers, 135
    Root Beer Chicken Wings, 47
    Slow Cooked Honey Garlic
        Chicken Thighs, 129
    Thai Chicken and Noodles, 139
    Thai Chicken Rice Bowls, 141
    White Chicken Chili, 89
Chicken Broccoli and Rice, 143
Chicken Cheddar Broccoli
    Soup, 55
Chicken Noodle Soup, 61
chicken sausage
    Split Pea Soup with Chicken
        Sausage, 73
Chicken Vegetable Soup, 59
Chicken with Lemon, 127
Chicken with Spiced Sesame
    Sauce, 145
chickpeas
    Hummus, 37
Chocolate Pots de Crème, 203
Cider, 219
Cinnamon French Toast
    Casserole, 25
cinnamon rolls
    Quick and Easy Instant Pot
        Cinnamon Rolls, 27

cloves
    Apple Butter, 23
coconut
    Fruit Breakfast Cobbler, 15
coconut milk
    Creamy Rice Pudding, 213
    Mild Chicken Curry with
        Coconut Milk, 147
Cookies & Cream Cheesecake
    (Gluten-Free), 206–207
corn
    Chicken Vegetable Soup, 59
    Potato and Corn Chowder, 93
    White Chicken Chili, 89
couscous
    Israeli couscous, 195
cranberries
    Baked Apples, 215
    Orange-Honey Cranberry
        Sauce, 199
    Quinoa with Almonds and
        Cranberries, 197
cream cheese
    Cookies & Cream Cheesecake
        (Gluten-Free), 206–207
    Creamy Chicken Wild Rice
        Soup, 57
    Creamy Spinach Dip, 41
    Spinach and Artichoke Dip, 39
Creamy Chicken Wild Rice
    Soup, 57
Creamy Jalapeño Dip, 43
Creamy Rice Pudding, 213
Creamy Spinach Dip, 41
Cynthia's Yogurt, 17

D
Daddy's Pasta Fasool, 155
Dump Cake, 205

E
eggs
    Cinnamon French Toast
        Casserole, 25

Instant Pot Hard-Boiled Eggs, 9
Poached Eggs, 11

F
Favorite Chili, 91
flaxseed
    Fruit Breakfast Cobbler, 15
Fruit Breakfast Cobbler, 15

G
garbanzo beans
    Hummus, 37
Garlic Galore Rotisserie
    Chicken, 121
ginger
    Candied Pecans, 35
green beans
    Chicken Vegetable Soup, 59
green chilies
    White Chicken Chili, 89
green pepper
    Favorite Chili, 91
    Ground Turkey Stew, 83
    Philly Cheese Steaks, 103
Ground Turkey Cacciatore
    Spaghetti, 153
Ground Turkey Stew, 83

H
ham
    Old Fashioned Ham 'n'
        Beans, 173
    Split Pea Soup, 69
hoisin sauce
    Teriyaki Ribs, 119
Honey Lemon Garlic Salmon,
    159
hot sauce
    Chicken Cheddar Broccoli
        Soup, 55
Hummus, 37

I
Instant Pot Applesauce, 21

Instant Pot Hard-Boiled Eggs, 9
Insta Pasta à la Maria, 137
Insta Popcorn, 33
Israeli couscous, 195
Italian dressing mix
    Philly Cheese Steaks, 103

J
jalapeño
    Creamy Jalapeño Dip, 43

K
kale
    Beef and Kale Stew, 87
    Kid-Friendly Mac & Cheese
        with Kale, 157
Kid-Friendly Mac & Cheese with
    Kale, 157

L
Lemony Chicken Thighs, 131
lentils
    Brown Lentil Soup, 77
lima beans
    Chicken Vegetable Soup, 59

M
maple syrup
    Candied Pecans, 35
    Fruit Breakfast Cobbler, 15
Mashed Potatoes, 175
mayonnaise
    Spinach and Artichoke Dip, 39
Meatball and Pasta Soup, 67
meatballs
    Meatball and Pasta Soup, 67
Meatballs, 49
Mild Chicken Curry with
    Coconut Milk, 147
molasses
    Baked Navy Beans, 167
    Steamed Brown Bread, 29
mushrooms
    Beef and Kale Stew, 87

Beef Stew, 84–85
Cheesy Stuffed Cabbage, 149
Creamy Chicken Wild Rice
    Soup, 57
Ground Turkey Cacciatore
    Spaghetti, 153
Insta Pasta à la Maria, 137

N
noodles
    Asian Chicken Noodle Soup,
        63
    Chicken Noodle Soup, 61
    Daddy's Pasta Fasool, 155
    Ground Turkey Cacciatore
        Spaghetti, 153
    Insta Pasta à la Maria, 137
    Kid-Friendly Mac & Cheese
        with Kale, 157
    Meatball and Pasta Soup, 67
    Thai Chicken and Noodles, 139
nutmeg
    Candied Pecans, 35

O
oats
    Fruit Breakfast Cobbler, 15
    steel-cut
        Best Steel Cut-Oats, 13
        Taylor's Favorite Uniquely
            Stuffed Peppers, 151
Old Fashioned Ham 'n'
    Beans, 173
orange
    Cider, 219
Orange Chicken Breasts, 133
Orange Chicken Thighs with
    Bell Peppers, 135
Orange-Honey Cranberry
    Sauce, 199
P
pasta. *See* noodles
peaches
    Fruit Breakfast Cobbler, 15

peanut butter
    Thai Chicken Rice Bowls, 141
pears
    Fruit Breakfast Cobbler, 15
peas
    Beef Stew, 84–85
    Chicken Noodle Soup, 61
    Chicken Vegetable Soup, 59
    Split Pea Soup, 69
    Split Pea Soup with Chicken
        Sausage, 73
    sugar snap
        Thai Chicken and Noodles,
          139
pecans
    Candied Pecans, 35
    Fruit Breakfast Cobbler, 15
Perfect Basmati Rice, 189
Perfect Sweet Potatoes, 183
Perfect White Rice, 185
Philippine Ulam, 113
Philly Cheese Steaks, 103
pie filling
    Dump Cake, 205
Poached Eggs, 11
popcorn
    Insta Popcorn, 33
Porcupine Meatballs, 51
pork
    BBQ Pork Sandwiches, 111
    Philippine Ulam, 113
    Pulled Pork, 109
Pork Baby Back Ribs, 117
Pork Butt Roast, 107
Potato and Corn Chowder, 93
Potato Bacon Soup, 71
potatoes
    Bacon Ranch Red Potatoes, 179
    Beef and Kale Stew, 87
    Beef Stew, 84–85
    Mashed Potatoes, 175
    Philippine Ulam, 113
    Pot Roast, 99
Potatoes with Parsley, 177

Potato Soup, 75
Pot Roast, 99
Pulled Pork, 109

Q
Quick and Easy Instant Pot
    Cinnamon Rolls, 27
Quick Steak Tacos, 97
Quinoa with Almonds and
    Cranberries, 197

R
raisins
    Best Steel Cut-Oats, 13
    golden
        Creamy Rice Pudding, 213
        Steamed Brown Bread, 29
ranch dressing mix
    Bacon Ranch Red Potatoes, 179
red bell pepper, 83
    Asian Chicken Noodle Soup,
        63
    Chicken Cheddar Broccoli
        Soup, 55
    Philly Cheese Steaks, 103
    Taylor's Favorite Uniquely
        Stuffed Peppers, 151
ribs
    Pork Baby Back Ribs, 117
    Tender Tasty Ribs, 115
rice
    Bell Pepper Casserole, 105
    Best Brown Rice, 191
    Brown Rice, 193
    Buttery Rice Pudding, 211
    Chicken Broccoli and Rice, 143
    Creamy Chicken Wild Rice
        Soup, 57
    Creamy Rice Pudding, 213
    Perfect Basmati Rice, 189
    Perfect White Rice, 185
    Porcupine Meatballs, 51
    Thai Chicken Rice Bowls, 141
    Unstuffed Cabbage Soup, 65

Rice Guiso, 187
Rice Pudding, 209
root beer
    Root Beer Chicken Wings, 47
Root Beer Chicken Wings, 47
S
salmon
    Honey Lemon Garlic Salmon,
        159
salsa
    Quick Steak Tacos, 97
sausage
    Polish
        Best Baked Beans, 170–171
        Split Pea Soup with Chicken
          Sausage, 73
    Taylor's Favorite Uniquely
        Stuffed Peppers, 151
Simple Salted Carrots, 163
Slow Cooked Honey Garlic
    Chicken Thighs, 129
sour cream
    Black Bean Soup, 81
    Creamy Jalapeño Dip, 43
    Creamy Spinach Dip, 41
    Potato Bacon Soup, 71
    Potato Soup, 75
    Quick Steak Tacos, 97
    Spinach and Artichoke Dip,
        39
    White Chicken Chili, 89
soy sauce
    Asian Chicken Noodle Soup,
        63
    Beef Broccoli, 101
    Beef Stew, 84–85
    Chicken with Spiced Sesame
        Sauce, 145
    Orange Chicken Breasts, 133
    Philippine Ulam, 113
    Slow Cooked Honey Garlic
        Chicken Thighs, 129
    Thai Chicken and Noodles,
        139

Thai Chicken Rice Bowls, 141
spinach
    Creamy Spinach Dip, 41
    Kid-Friendly Mac & Cheese
        with Kale, 157
Spinach and Artichoke Dip, 39
Split Pea Soup, 69
Split Pea Soup with Chicken
    Sausage, 73
squash
    Butternut Squash Soup, 79
sriracha sauce
    Teriyaki Ribs, 119
    Thai Chicken Rice Bowls, 141
Steamed Brown Bread, 29
sweet potato
    Chicken Vegetable Soup, 59
    Perfect Sweet Potatoes, 183
Sweet Potato Puree, 181

T
tacos
    Quick Steak Tacos, 97
tahini
    Chicken with Spiced Sesame
        Sauce, 145
    Hummus, 37

Taylor's Favorite Uniquely
    Stuffed Peppers, 151
Tender Tasty Ribs, 115
Teriyaki Ribs, 119
Thai Chicken and Noodles, 139
Thai Chicken Rice Bowls, 141
tomatoes
    Bell Pepper Casserole, 105
    Butter Chicken, 123
    Chicken Vegetable Soup, 59
    Daddy's Pasta Fasool, 155
    Favorite Chili, 91
    Mild Chicken Curry with
        Coconut Milk, 147
    Unstuffed Cabbage Soup, 65
tomato sauce
    Bell Pepper Casserole, 105
    Cheesy Stuffed Cabbage, 149
    Daddy's Pasta Fasool, 155
    Ground Turkey Cacciatore
        Spaghetti, 153
    Ground Turkey Stew, 83
    Insta Pasta à la Maria, 137
    Meatballs, 49
tomato soup
    Porcupine Meatballs, 51
tortillas

Quick Steak Tacos, 97
turkey
    Cheesy Stuffed Cabbage, 149
    Ground Turkey Cacciatore
        Spaghetti, 153
    Ground Turkey Stew, 83
    Porcupine Meatballs, 51
    Unstuffed Cabbage Soup, 65

U
Unstuffed Cabbage Soup, 65

W
White Chicken Chili, 89

Y
yogurt
    Black Bean Soup, 81
    Carol's Yogurt, 19
    Cynthia's Yogurt, 17

Z
zucchini
    Taylor's Favorite Uniquely
        Stuffed Peppers, 151

About the Author

Hope Comerford is a mom, wife, elementary music teacher, blogger, recipe developer, public speaker, ALM Zone fit leader, Young Living Essential Oils enthusiast/educator, and published author. In 2013, she was diagnosed with a severe gluten intolerance and since then has spent many hours creating easy, practical and delicious gluten-free recipes that can be enjoyed by both those who are affected by gluten and those who are not.

Growing up, Hope spent many hours in the kitchen with her Meme (grandmother) and her love for cooking grew from there. While working on her master's degree when her daughter was young, Hope turned to her slow cookers for some salvation and sanity. It was from there she began truly experimenting with recipes and quickly learned she had the ability to get a little more creative in the kitchen and develop her own recipes.

In 2010, Hope started her blog, *A Busy Mom's Slow Cooker Adventures*, to simply share the recipes she was making with her family and friends. She never imagined people all over the world would begin visiting her page and sharing her recipes with others as well. In 2013, Hope self-published her first cookbook, *Slow Cooker Recipes 10 Ingredients or Less and Gluten-Free*, and then later wrote *The Gluten-Free Slow Cooker*.

Hope became the new brand ambassador and author of Fix-It and Forget-It in mid-2016. Since then, she has brought her excitement and creativeness to the Fix-It and Forget-It brand. Through Fix-It and Forget-It, she has written *Fix-It and Forget-It Lazy and Slow, Fix-It and Forget-It Healthy Slow Cooker Cookbook, Fix-It and Forget-It Favorite Slow Cooker Recipes for Mom, Fix-It and Forget-It Favorite Slow Cooker Recipes for Dad, Welcome Home Cookbook, Fix-It and Forget-It Holiday Favorites, Fix-It and Forget-It Cooking for Two, Fix-It and Forget-It Slow Cooker Crowd Pleasers for the American Summer, Fix-It and Forget-It Slow Cooker Dump Dinners and Desserts, Welcome Home Diabetic Cookbook*, and *Welcome Home Harvest Cookbook*.

Hope lives in the city of Clinton Township, Michigan, near Metro Detroit. She's a native of Michigan and has lived there her whole life. She has been happily married to her husband and best friend, Justin, since 2008. Together they have two children, Ella and Gavin, who are her motivation, inspiration, and heart. In her spare time, Hope enjoys traveling, singing, cooking, reading books, spending time with friends and family, and relaxing.

FIX-IT and FORGET-IT®

FIX-IT and FORGET-IT®
NEW COOKBOOK

250 new delicious slow cooker recipes!

New York Times bestselling author

Phyllis Good

New York Times bestselling author **Phyllis Good**

FIX-IT and FORGET-IT®
BAKING with your SLOW COOKER

150 Slow Cooker Recipes for Breads, Pizza, Cakes, Tarts, Crisps, Bars, Pies, Cupcakes, and More!

FIX-IT and FORGET-IT®
Lazy AND Slow COOKBOOK

365 Days of SLOW COOKER Recipes

HOPE COMERFORD

NEW YORK TIMES BESTSELLING SERIES

FIX-IT and FORGET-IT® Healthy
SLOW COOKER COOKBOOK

New York Times Bestselling Series

150 Whole Food Recipes for Paleo, Vegan, Gluten-Free, and Diabetic-Friendly Diets
HOPE COMERFORD

NEW YORK TIMES BESTSELLING SERIES
FIX-IT and FORGET-IT®

FAVORITE **SLOW COOKER** RECIPES FOR **MOM**

150 RECIPES MOM WILL LOVE TO MAKE, EAT, AND SHARE!
HOPE COMERFORD

NEW YORK TIMES BESTSELLING SERIES
FIX-IT and FORGET-IT®

FAVORITE **SLOW COOKER** RECIPES FOR **DAD**

150 RECIPES DAD WILL LOVE TO MAKE, EAT, AND SHARE!
HOPE COMERFORD

Fix-It and FORGET-It®
SLOW COOKER
DUMP DINNERS
AND DESSERTS

150 CRAZY YUMMY MEALS
FOR YOUR CRAZY BUSY LIFE

NEW YORK
TIMES
BESTSELLING
SERIES

HOPE COMERFORD

NEW YORK TIMES BESTSELLING SERIES
Fix-It and FORGET-It®
COOKING FOR TWO

150 SMALL-BATCH
SLOW COOKER RECIPES

HOPE COMERFORD

NEW YORK TIMES BESTSELLING SERIES
Fix-It and FORGET-It®
Holiday Favorites

150 EASY AND DELICIOUS Slow Cooker RECIPES

Hope Comerford

#1 New York Times bestseller!
MORE THAN 5 million COPIES ALREADY SOLD!

Fix-It and FORGET-It®
Cookbook
REVISED & UPDATED
700 Great Slow Cooker Recipes

Phyllis Pellman Good

Fix-It and FORGET-It®
kids' Cookbook

By the New York Times Bestselling Author

50 Favorite Recipes to Make in a Slow Cooker
Phyllis Pellman Good

Mac and Cheese
Tacos
Chocolate Pudding Cake

NEW YORK TIMES BESTSELLING SERIES
Fix-It and FORGET-It®
★★★★★★
CROWD PLEASERS
FOR THE AMERICAN SUMMER

150 FAVORITE SLOW COOKER RECIPES
FOR POTLUCKS, PARTIES, AND FAMILY GATHERINGS

HOPE COMERFORD

By *The New York Times* bestselling author

FIX-IT and FORGET-IT

5-ingredient favorites

Comforting *Slow-Cooker* Recipes

Phyllis Pellman Good

By the *New York Times* bestselling author

FIX-IT and FORGET-IT

BOX SET

A $47.85 VALUE!

PHYLLIS GOOD

By the *New York Times* Bestselling Author

FIX-IT and FORGET-IT

Slow Cooker Magic

550 Amazing Everyday Recipes

Phyllis Good

By the *New York Times* Bestselling Author

FIX-IT and FORGET-IT

Vegetarian Cookbook

565 Delicious Slow-Cooker, Stove-Top, Oven, and Salad Recipes, plus 50 Suggested Menus

Also for cooks wanting to make more meatless meals!

Phyllis Good

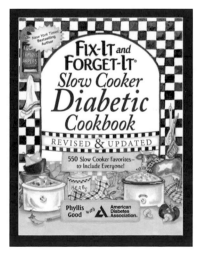

New York Times Bestselling Authors

FIX-IT and FORGET-IT

Slow Cooker Diabetic Cookbook

REVISED & UPDATED

550 Slow Cooker Favorites— to Include Everyone!

Phyllis Good with American Diabetes Association.

New York Times Bestseller!

More Than 1,200,000 Copies Sold!

FIX-IT and FORGET-IT

Cooking Light for Slow Cookers

REVISED & UPDATED

600 Healthy, Low-Fat Recipes for Your Slow Cooker

Phyllis Good

UPCOMING BOOKS FROM

FIX-IT AND FORGET-IT

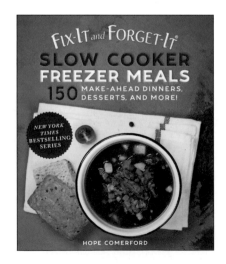

ALSO BY HOPE COMERFORD

Welcome Home
COOKBOOK SERIES